THE
ANATOMY
OF A
GOALKEEPER

WRITTEN BY ADAM WOODAGE

INTERVIEW LIST:

MAX CROCOMBE (NEW ZEALAND U23 GK)

MAGNUS KLEY (PROGKTRAINING)

ADRIAN MOLLER (PROGKTRAINING)

MELISSA BARBIERI (AUSTRALIA WOMEN'S CAPTAIN)

ERIC KLENOFSKY (TOP USA COLLEGE GK)

WAYNE BROWN (OXFORD UNITED GOALKEEPER COACH)

RICHARD LEE (EX-BPL GK & ENTREPRENEUR)

CASPER ANKERGREN (BRIGHTON & HOVE ALBION GK)

JON HORTON (WELSH WOMEN'S GOALKEEPER COACH)

TONY ELLIOTT (ENGLAND FUTSAL GOALKEEPER COACH)

NICK LEVETT (THE FA NATIONAL TALENT ID MANAGER)

OLIVER MARTIN (NON-LEAGUE AND EX-ACADEMY GK)

MATT CAMPBELL (BLACKBURN ROVERS SCHOLAR)

DEAN THORNTON (QPR ACADEMY GOALKEEPER COACH)

BEN FRANKS (COACHING DEGREE GRADUATE)

BOBBY WHITE (LONDON 2012 HANDBALL CAPTAIN)

MICK PAYNE (ENGLAND C TEAM GOALKEEPER COACH)

RICH O'DONNELL (BRISTOL CITY GK)

SCOTT DALY (OXFORD UNITED SPORTS SCIENTIST)

THOMAS DENNIS (ENGLAND FUTSAL GK)

GLOVEGLU (LATEX PRODUCT)

CRAZY CATCH (REBOUND NETS)

REUSCH (GERMAN GLOVE BRAND)

HO SOCCER (SPANISH AND PORTUGESE GLOVE BRAND)

ONE SPORT (BRITISH GLOVE BRAND)

JUST4KEEPERS (GOALKEEPER COACHING SCHOOL)

Written by: Adam Woodage
Design: Adam Woodage
Editing: Rob Paripovic
Covers: Miklos Zsengeller
Printed and bound by: GOMER Printing

ISBN: 978-0-9935165-9-7

A catalogue record for this book is available from the British Library.

WITH THANKS TO...

A massive thank you to everybody who was involved in the project. They didn't have to, but they did anyway:

- GLOVE GLU (OUR PRINCIPAL SPONSORS!)

- GK ICON

- THE PFA

- OUR INTERVIEW TEAM

- MURSLEY UNITED FC

- GOMER PRINTING

- REUSCH AND HO SOCCER (BOOK PHOTOS)

- OSCAR COLE

- MIKLOS ZSENGELLER

- LIAT HUGHES JOSHI

- ROB PARIPOVIC

- MYLES BOWMAN

- LUKE PRIESTLEY AND MICHAEL ROUSELL

- SAM HEASMAN

- GREG BROOKHOUSE

- BEN COLDICOTT

- JACK BRONZE

PHOTO NOTICE...

To the best of our knowledge, all photos contained within this book are either of the property of those interviewed or with their permission and right to be reproduced within this publication (with the exception of the full-page spreads, within which the photos have been supplied by Reusch and HO Soccer).

Every effort has been made to trace and contact copyright holders where applicable. If there are any inadvertent omissions we apologise to those concerned, and ask that you contact us so that we can correct any oversight as soon as possible. The contact details are given below:

The Anatomy of a Goalkeeper
6 Chaffinch
Watermead
Aylesbury
Bucks
HP19 0GQ

We thank you for your cooperation and understanding within this matter.

OC1

THE JOURNEY SO FAR...

ADAM WOODAGE

There is absolutely no doubt in my mind that this project has only been possible due to the willing, initiative and pure passion for the world of goalkeeping, coaching and football as a whole exhibited not only by our incredible interview team but also those who have given up their time to move the project forward as a whole.

It seems an age ago that the initial idea for the project was conceived. If I recall correctly, I was actually sat in a dinner party at the time and (rudely, for sure!) checking an incoming message on my iPad. It was this initial discussion with a friend of mine that I hold in the highest of regards that the nucleus of the book was formed.

From there, it was a matter of moulding, remoulding and then maybe tweaking a little more. We discovered that what we really needed was something that could reach out not just the inter-connected world of goalkeeper coaches but also to the footballing community as a whole, providing some sort of insight to the mysterious, lonely and yet undeniably incredible position that the goalkeeper holds.

Distilling this ignorant stigma and yet instilling the hope and celebration of the Goalkeeper Union was never set to be an easy task for a couple of teenagers. The authority required to write such a controversial and hopefully thought-provoking book is understandably absent from the arsenal of a 16-year-old school student.

However, it would transpire to be the support, dedication and unrelenting desire to share knowledge of the world of goalkeeping that would allow us to unlock the door to this abundant fountain of perspective, experiences and opinions, where every goalkeeper has their own individual stories, techniques and ideas as to how they reached the level they are at today.

It is incredibly humbling that such a vast majority of this world chose to share their story with us.

If I am to recall my personal journey, executing these interviews, over the past couple of months especially, it makes for a rollercoaster journey across the country and a plethora of different venues. Every interview has been different: we are lucky enough to be able to draw on the thoughts and words of athletes from all across the world, from Denmark to Australia and back via the USA! It is not just the physical locations of our interviewees that have given such breadth to the whole project, though, but their roles, positions and past experiences, too.

Having the honour of sitting down over lunch

with the likes of The FA's National Talent ID Manager Nick Levett in itself added so much extra audacity and weight to the coaching elements of the book, whilst conversations with Rich Lee, Melissa Barbieri and Wayne Brown gave us some incredible stories that we can now take forward and share with the goalkeeping world.

Writing this short extract, though, feels almost immoral without mention of each and every interviewee who literally went the extra mile not just to answer the questions that were posed with the full force of their past experiences but also in support of the book and its subsequent distribution to the goalkeeping world otherwise, whether through advice, building on contacts or actively sharing the progress themselves.

As I have said, a huge thank you is in order for that. It is most humbling and supportive of the goalkeeping world, especially from those interviewees who may not have any natural connection to the sport.

To be totally honest with you, as the reader, the journey feels as though it has only just begun. I sit here, writing, on July 16th, one day before we send the book to print and the evening of returning from an absolutely incredible week on pre-season tour with Oxford United (yes: that does explain the club's random bias in the book!) and I truly believe that this is only the start of what is to follow.

In order for this to flourish, though, and the opinions within these white pages shared to the degree that they will make huge shifts to the goalkeeping world, we need your help.

All along, this has been a mission of camaraderie, teamwork and togetherness. Now, though, as we move forward to the realisation of our initial ideas, we are under no illusions that there will be unfound errors in our plans that could undo all of the incredible hard work that has preceded it.

We can, however, combat this, working as a union of goalkeepers dedicated not just to improving the quality of those we're producing between the sticks, but also educating the rest of the footballing world as to their importance and encouraging the further celebration of the goalkeeper union.

Whether it be something as simple as sharing the book onto your social media pages, discussing the idea with any potential contacts who might be disposed to push the book further or even just getting in touch to give us your feedback about the project, every action you take is a very tangible one and will have a real difference on producing the next generation of goalkeepers and educating coaches in a meantime.

On behalf of everyone who has been involved with the project to whatever degree, I thank you for taking the time out of our coaching or playing schedule to have a read through some of what these truly incredible academics, coaches, goalkeepers and industry experts have to say.

It is testament to their words that we have a book here today that you have decided to look a little deeper at and I sincerely promise that there is an abundance of hidden coaching, playing and development gems for anyone in the world of football to pick up.

From me, all I say is that I wish you all the best in your future goalkeeping experiences and that maybe, in one way or another, this book can return its value to you in the quality of advice, perspective and insight it throws across.

Yours in goalkeeping,

Adam.

Twitter: @adamwoodage
Instagram: @wwwadamwoodagecom
Snapchat: adamwoodage.com
Website: www.adamwoodage.com
Email: adam@fifawithoutlimits.com

Please feel free to get in touch!

GLOBAL GOALKEEPING

From debuts across the world to representing your country at a height of 168cm, our first book section is jam-packed with an abundance of hilarious, insightful and entertaining stories into the world of the professional goalkeepers who we watch and analyse so heavily. A little lighter, perhaps, than the rest of the book... But still with some interesting and unheard of facets!!

ONCE A KIWI, ALWAYS A KIWI

MAX CROCOMBE

Eligible to play for a variety of national teams including Australia, England and Switzerland, there was no decision for a young Max Crocombe to make when the opportunity came about to represent his birth country of New Zealand. He shares his stories, experiences and memories from his game-time so far and the different dynamics of the game in New Zealand.

How did the opportunity to play for the New Zealand national team come about?

I'm a kiwi, through and through. I was born in New Zealand, as were part of my family and that is what I identify myself as.

I have played in the U20s and U23s, with about a dozen appearances on the bench for the first team, too. I think that I've played well through the majority of the times I've been out there, but of course there are a couple of occasions that don't go quite to plan...

I think, actually, the U20s World Cup in 2013 was my worst. In the first game, I miskicked a ball to the opposing striker and he broke through and scored.

After that, I had loads of people criticising me and telling me that I wasn't ready for the first team yet which is a shame because I believe I

had quite a good tournament other than that. But, at the end of the day, if you make a mistake in football that's what you've almost got to expect and learn to deal with.

What are the different dynamics in playing for New Zealand?

I always love going away with my country, and especially look forward to the FIFA windows where I have the opportunity to represent the Silver Fern.

Qualifying for major tournaments through the age groups has been challenging, from U20s to the senior side. Teams in Oceania are very competitive, talented and athletic, particularly as the conditions tend to suit the home nations who are more used to the heat and humidity, compared to most of our squads living further away from the equator!

It's incredible how quick and powerful some of the players we face are and often the Oceanic nations don't get the credit they deserve generally because of the FIFA rankings.

I was on the bench for our OFC Nations Cup 2016 victory this summer and in the final we faced Papua New Guinea, the hosts, and at 120 minutes in 32 degree heat they'd only made one sub and their players didn't even look to be tiring!

What's the infrastructure of these kinds of tournaments like?

Like I said, the standard of everything is improving and that includes the infrastructure. There have been a few what I would call, 'different' training grounds, though...

With the U20s in Fiji in 2013 for our World Cup qualifiers, our training setup was on a patch of grass behind the rooms at our hotel and even had a few frogs trying to playing with us, too! Additionally, the U23s in Papa New Guinea for the Olympic qualifiers in 2015 were equally eye-opening:

The first day we trained on a local patch of what looked like just flat terrain, with enormous cracks running through the middle of it because it was so dry... This was in the wet season, supposedly!

The coaches, of course, were very cautious about risking injuries so it did limit us to what we could do but I just remember getting the balls out and nobody could control them because they were just bobbling over their feet. These were really good players looking like they'd never touched a football in their life!

For the second day, we trained opposite a local school, a few miles away from our hotel, and there was absolutely no grass on this pitch: just solid ground and goals with no nets. It was obviously well below our expectations for a training facility but looking across into the school became a very sobering experience and one that really put everything that we were doing into context.

Every single person there will tell you how much it resonated with them, and just how lucky we are in the lives we live back home.

Recently, though, the facilities have improved a lot and the training pitches we used last summer in the Nations Cup were good whilst the pitches we've played on for matches have never been an issue.

What's the quality of the New Zealand squad like and where do they play?

The quality of the squad is good. I like the goalkeepers that I work with, they're first class. We've always had good goalkeepers through the age groups and this stands us in good stead moving forward.

In England, we're so lucky that we have so many different tiers and levels of football where the standard is still really good.

A lot of the players play abroad from New

Zealand, probably about half of them. The New Zealand league is a decent standard, it's semi-professional, and then you have Wellington Phoenix who play in the Australian A-League, flying over for away games and vice-versa. Phoenix are basically the hotbed for New Zealand talent, with the chance to move further into the A-League and this is especially prevalent now as they've just had their licence renewed.

Of course, there are players scattered around all of Europe and Austalia, a lot of really good players that have their own, unique qualities.

Do you have to change the way you play at all when playing for New Zealand?

Generally, I like to keep my style pretty consistent and not change it too much because it's always been my belief that I'll play my best when I'm following my own mind-set. There has been a contrast, however, in the past between New Zealand and England, probably because with New Zealand, the teams we have played against have tended to sit off more so there's been more time on the ball and more opportunities to play out which is encouraged and I enjoy.

In England, certainly I found in the National League, the teams are more inclined to win the ball back quickly and will close you down when the ball's at your feet so, especially in the winter when the quality of the pitches deteriorate, it's smarter to just play that bit more direct and hit bigger balls into the front players.

Tell us about the photo of you at Barnet... That's a bit of a special one, right?

Haha. I signed for Barnet for a month, on loan, and on our first day at training we're just doing our normal small-sided games. I looked up across the scenery, above the pitches and to, sort of, a large fence where there is this huge New Zealand flag which has been posted up.

I asked one of the lads I was training with who it was for, wondering what sort of the connections the club might have, and he

basically explained that it was probably for me...

It turns out that there was this huge Barnet fan who absolutely loves the club, stood next to the flag.

He has no connection to New Zealand but runs the Barnet fans' group so I went up after the training session just to say hello. I just said "Alright mate, thanks for the flag! That's a lovely gesture". He explained that it was no problem and asked for a photo with me, to be taken by one of the other lads who were training at the time...

For your first day at a new club it's pretty nice. I can't say I've ever been welcomed quite like that before!!

THE NORWEGIAN YOUTUBERS...

MAGNUS KLEY & ADRIAN MØLLER

We are consistently being told of the wonderful world of social media, the internet and the ultra-connected technologies that we're living in. For goalkeepers, this opens up a wealth of knowledge, experience and innovative drills that coaches and players can take to their sessions from all over the globe. We speak to Norwegian goalkeepers Magnus Kley and Adrian Jonuzi Møller on their background, their YouTube and Instagram channels and their plans moving forward...

How did you both get into football and, more specifically, goalkeeping?

Interestingly, the two of us had very different pathways into football:

Adrian started as a little boy, (just 5 or 6 years old) playing much more out on pitch, before he started in goal as a 12-year-old. Magnus was not that interested in football as a young child and was switching a lot between various sports before he finally got into football properly. With sports like judo, swimming and skiing taking the forefront, he started playing as a goalkeeper at 11 years of age, after one year of playing out on pitch.

From here on, we played football together for many years. Adrian played matches for his own team, but also trained up a

year with Magnus' team, who were a year older. Because of this, we were able to train together on a very regular basis, developing a good and solid friendship as well as efficient and competitive training routines as we were both vying for that No1 spot.

After some time, when we both were older, Magnus moved to Vålerenga Oslo, which is one of the top clubs in the Norwegian League.

He played here for a year and a half, from about the age of 16, mingling with many Norwegian talents, before returning to his mother club, Skeid, and playing here through the rest of the youth ladder.

At Skeid, we had to compete fiercely with each other in training to secure our places but our friendship was never affected; we were always fair towards each other.

Later, Adrian moved to another club and then went on to get a professional contract at Vålerenga, where he is still playing today, currently in his second year and having had an incredibly strong start to his career so far.

He has received much deserved attention for his willingness to train, to remain disciplined and his general mind-set, which led to him having the opportunity to play in a friendly match against Real Madrid, at the tender age

of 19, in front of 27,000 fans at the Ullevål Stadium.

This was a terrific experience, meeting players like Navas, Bale, Kroos, Rodriguez and other big stars, as well as an opportunity for Adrian to really put himself in the spotlight of major clubs.

Magnus, on the other hand, is still struggling with a recurring knee injury, picked up at the start of the 2015/16 season. Because of this, he has to be very careful with his knee and therefore he is spending a lot more time with strength and conditioning coaches and therapists, but hopes to be moving back into the game in search of a club over the ensuing weeks and months.

If it transpires that professional football will not be an option, this will be no hindrance to Magnus, though, as he seeks to obtain his UEFA coaching qualifications and continues his studies in physiotherapy and personal training.

How does goalkeeping in Norway compare to how we see it in the UK?

To be honest, neither of us are big believers in Norwegian goalkeeper training. The footballing system in Norway isn't as professional as in England, Germany, Italy or Spain. It is amateur in comparison, especially for the younger teams and as a goalkeeper.

Many teams only have goalkeeper coaches for the first team and maybe the junior teams up from around the U14 level, so many goalkeepers wait a particularly long time before they get any good goalkeeper training or a coach.

It tends to be only the very best clubs in the country with goalkeeper coaches for all the goalkeepers and these can still be hit and miss sometimes, anyway. In our experience, we have seen maybe two or three really good quality coaches over the last 10 years, whereas we've worked with a good dozen or so in total.

Looking back on it, we were so lucky to have each other to train with and I think this may be a big part in what has helped us develop to where we are today and certainly for Adrian, now playing at a top level, with regular, quality goalkeeper coaching.

So, breaking it down, what are the issues with Norwegian goalkeeping?

The goalkeeper training in Norway is very plain. It focuses a lot on shot stopping and reactions, but often coaches won't focus on important techniques (grip, balance, positioning), as well as the physical aspects like coordination and power.

When you combine this with the lack of game-based scenarios goalkeepers are often trained in, we can start to see the issues with Norwegian goalkeeping and why there are, maybe, fewer goalkeepers that have been produced from the country in comparison to its Scandinavian counterparts.

You can see the difference much more patently in videos from goalkeepers in England, Germany, Spain and Italy especially. There is a much wider variety of drills and exercises used, with a greater influence on the facets aforementioned.

Are there any other things that you think might have influenced the game?

We think sports like handball have had a huge influence on the goalkeeping game, especially in the countries where it is so popular like mainland Europe.

Handball goalkeepers tend to be much more flexible and have quicker reactions due to the nature of the shots from closer range and the need to use your legs in a much more explosive and flexible way compared to football.

On the other hand, though, it can also be a disadvantage at times as the goalkeeper gets used to the smaller-sized goal or starts to over-anticipate shots by diving too early, as they may do to good effect in handball. We don't know so much about handball (football has always been our first sport!), but it's clear that top goalkeepers have taken inspiration from there.

If you watch Manuel Neuer closely in a one-on-one situation, he often jumps out with his legs and arms like a handball goalkeeper. It almost looks like he's imitating a starfish, with all his arms and legs out to the side and employing the common blocking techniques that have become much more prevalent recently.

After his recognition as one of the world's best goalkeepers, more and more football goalkeepers have started to do the same. It is a clearly inspiration from handball and I think we see this very obviously in Norway, too!

How does the standard of the Norwegian top-league compare to England for goalkeeping?

As we have said, the level in England is much higher. The interest for football is also on a whole different level. In Norway, there isn't much interest in the Norwegian League like in Europe. Understandably (due to the low level of football), many Norwegians will support and follow the big European clubs, especially the big BPL teams, and not really take too much interest in their own league.

The Norwegian national team doesn't play very successfully, either, so the attention is mainly directed towards English clubs here in Norway! Most popular are clearly Manchester United and Liverpool, but Chelsea don't lie too far away these days...

You're currently involved with a variety of YouTube videos showcasing some of the professional goalkeeper training that you've had. How did the idea for this come about?

The account actually started from our own inspiration that we were taking from European training videos that we would then implement within our routines. We have always found them to be particularly insightful and, from the age of about 12 years old, we were doing drills we could never have dreamed of doing at our own club.

This, coupled with biographies from the likes of Jens Lehmann and videos from Andreas Köpke (German National Team Goalkeeper Coach) really cemented both the motivation to start making goalkeeper videos but also stimulated the content that we would provide to young goalkeepers, too.

Over time, we developed a really good

understanding of the kind of intensity that worked for sessions, as well as the different dynamics that we could tweak slightly to use the drill for our desired purpose and, most importantly, we had a strongly-held belief that our work was exciting and different from others of a similar type in Oslo and therefore we wanted to, and were committed to, showing that.

There are a lot of goalkeepers out there who struggle with poor training methods and little knowledge. To think that we could have impacted on just a small minority of this population in Norway is a very humbling and rewarding thought.

What sort of success are we talking about?

It was a huge success at first: we actually reached 230,000 views on our first video and this, of course, motivated us to make more.

Thanks to YouTube, we have had so much feedback from people and gotten to know people from all over the world who also have encouraged us to make more and we are much more confident that our videos now are considerably better than those when we started, at the young age of just 16 and 17.

The feedback we've had so far also catalysed us to make an Instagram profile to showcase our daily life as goalkeepers and athletes. YouTube has given us great experiences, contacts, jobs and new opportunities... Being able to be part of this book, for example, isn't a bad start!

Moving forward into the future, how would you like to develop the channel to grow your audience?

We have dedicated an awful lot of time to filming recently, in many different types of settings and trainings so be prepared for much variation in the future videos....

Additionally, most of the new videos feature a professional cameraman and, therefore, hopefully the videos will be much more exciting as well as informative for the viewer.

This also gave us the opportunity to focus 100% on the training while the cameraman did his job, which was hugely appreciated as normally we have had to make the videos ourselves at the same time!

We've got about 10 videos already filmed that we're yet to publish yet, including...

- **Motivational videos for goalkeepers**
- **Core training sessions**
- **Strength and coordination sessions**
- **A 'How to work out on holidays' guide***

*(which will show a workout on the beach shot on muscle beach in LA, I am told – not too bad eh!)

Now, then, what is the long-term plan for your YouTube channel and future careers?

Our main focus and goal for the channel will always be goalkeeper videos, but we have added new variations and new exercises as well as new types of filming and editing just to keep everything fresh.

Right now, for example, we are working on making a new channel trailer which will look much better and show more of our channel in addition to purchasing some shiny new cameras, meaning everything will be in HD from now on as oppose to before where some of the videos weren't of great quality!

We are certainly taking our YouTube channel much more seriously now and are experiencing considerably more success because of this. We've also been planning a video highlights reel from both of us for a while now, so maybe that will be something else the future holds!

You can find Magnus and Adrian's videos on YouTube under progktraining **and their Instagram profile is of the same name!**

THE CHALLENGE OF HEIGHT

MELISSA BARBIERI

It isn't uncommon at all to hear modern-day greats, such as Hugo Lloris or Iker Casillas defined as 'small' goalkeepers, in comparsion to the formidable frame of Fraser Forster, for example. However, ex-Australian international goalkeeper and captain Melissa Barbieri - who only became a goalkeeper in her early 20s - dispells this whole stigma, not because she's only just under that 5"10 mark (about average for a women's goalkeeper) but because she's 168cm tall, or 5"7 in old money:

Obviously a height of 168cm is not the tallest for a goalkeeper, how did you cope with this during the game?

When I played the game, I was known as the 'chess master'. I know the game really well and, where possible, I try to prevent saves before I have to make them.

Using my teammates and defenders, I'm able to get a lot of the dirty work done for me without having to make a save, because I understand the game so well in that sense and can instruct players to drop back, push forward and stand up attackers accordingly.

In saying that, though, I had no real problems reaching the top-corner shots either.

I had a vertical jump in the 50cms and, combined with the timing I picked up from playing basketball when I was younger, I found that I had an awful lot of those extra marginal gain '1%s', which would add up when it came down to it and see me making saves that maybe weren't proportionate to my height.

I also controlled my box very well, because I understood that height was a problem and so I really tried to dominate that and make attackers try something different to get the ball in there.

What about things like corners? Did you find yourself glued to your line or did you come out and try to get something on everything?

Because my timing was pretty good, I was in the position where I could try and come for most, if not all, crosses. It wasn't until later in my career that we had pretty good (and tall!) defenders, meaning I wouldn't need to do it so much, as they could deal with most of the stuff that was coming in.

Back in the day when we were doing a lot of man marking, I had the time and space to come and collect things but there was obviously then the transition to zonal marking and I would have big centre-halfs in front of me who would almost be an obstacle to getting the ball.

I definitely had to adjust at this point, spending more time picking and choosing which balls to come for.

Finally, what advice would you have for smaller goalkeepers looking to progress in the game?

For me, it's all about working on your vertical jump and making sure that you can get the ones that are unreachable for most people.

In order to achieve this, you need to be working on your timing, positioning and your footwork.

Quite often, a lot of the taller goalkeepers (with no disrespect) maybe don't value their agility and athleticism so highly, and so if you can concentrate on these areas of the game, you may see yourself starting to make the saves other goalkeepers are less inclined to make.

Starting position is another massive one for me. If you look at it, giving yourself a yard or two either forward or backward can be the make or break of whether you do or don't make a save, so it's certainly something that is worth playing around with.

A lot of the time people would say that I was too advanced as a goalkeeper, but this was how I felt it necessary to put pressure on the delivery coming in.

For example, if a free-kick was coming in, I might find myself standing around the penalty spot area, and they would very rarely put it into the middle because I'm there and waiting.

I guess it was that, even though I'm not particularly tall, there was the added element of intimidation and fear for the attacker that helped to keep the ball out of the box.

THE AMERICAN DREAM...

ERIC KLENOFSKY

Long gone are the days of American's striving to live off the fatta' the land, as Lennie would so blissfully put it in the great 'Of Mice and Men' novel. Away from the franchises of basketball, baseball and American football, 'soccer' is making a name for itself over in the US, too, with it recently being ranked the second most popular sport for the milennial generation. Top American college goalkeeper Eric Klenofsky fills us in with more details about his development so far as well as the general pathway across the pond:

You're career is going well at the moment and you're beginning to pick up some national recognition as a top-class college goalkeeper, how did you get to this point... What was your journey like?

I think when you talk about anyone's individual success story there are two key components:

The first being mentorship. I firmly believe that you are what you're exposed to and I think the mentors I've had throughout my life have really moulded my mind-set and moulded me into the person I am today.

The second key component is hard work. Whether you were born with all the God given talent in the world or you were born with barely enough to make it, I think at some point you need to put in the work and make the sacrifices to get to where you want to be in life.

For me, some of the most influential mentors I had, and still have, are my parents, along with all of the coaches at my youth club TSF Academy, specifically Steve Beneventine, Walter Gotrell, John Saunders, Andy Meaney, Luis Mendoza and Dan Christian.

Without playing at TSF Academy I would not be doing this interview right now because I would not be nearly the person I am today without them. The important thing to remember and something I think about often is that any success story is a step-by-step process: you have to go from point A to point B in order to get to point C and you can't go from A to C without B.

What I mean by this is that I couldn't go from my local town team as an 8-year-old to starting for a Division One university; I had to take steps to get there. The next step after TSF Academy was Monmouth University.

Monmouth has helped me not only mature on the field but also to grow up as an adult as well. The coaching staff at Monmouth have been so impactful in my life and I don't think that I would be as successful with any other group of coaches in the country.

Coach McCourt, Hugh MacDonald and Alex Blackburn have been integral in my development process.

Coach McCourt and Hughie have helped me grow up in terms of how I play and have also helped me learn the game. Blackburn is different, though: he's my goalkeeper coach, and who I'm closest with.

Blackburn really opened my eyes to a new way of goalkeeping when I got to Monmouth and I can't thank him enough for it. Without Blackburn's coaching abilities and knowledge of goalkeeping, I would be sitting on a bench somewhere trying to figure why I wasn't on the field and that's the truth.

Hard work is my next key component. I associate hard work with a mind-set. In order to engage in the consistent action it takes to achieve success, you have to have the correct mind-set to get you there.

Mental toughness is the name of the game in terms of goalkeeping. Walter Gotrell, my youth goalkeeper coach at TSF, Steve Beneventine, the owner of TSF, my high school coach, John Saunders, my old TSF coach and my mother all set the example of mental toughness and the correct mind-set to have when going about achieving your goals.

I think these people gave me the platform to

mould my thinking. I can remember being a 14-year-old and sitting in TSF with Walter and he was talking to me about how when he was my age and going into high school, he couldn't kick a ball. Because of that, he spent close to six or seven hours a day kicking balls until he felt comfortable enough with his distribution.

In my head, it gave me a clear pathway as to what I'd have to do next to achieve success. So, every chance I got, I was out at the park next to my house kicking balls trying to get

the backspin I wanted.

I'd be lying if I told you I'm not still working on it. But that's the level of commitment it takes to make your dreams a reality. You have to love what you're doing. That's the only way you can spend six hours a day kicking a ball.

That mind-set and that notion of hard work comes from the mentors I've been blessed with and so I am thankful to them for that.

How did playing with the New York Red Bulls U23 side this Summer compare to college football?

It was great to play for the New York Red Bulls this summer; I've never been on a team that has a professional club attached to it so it was really a dream come true to be a part of a really professional atmosphere like that.

I think it is difficult to compare college football to the PDL. For those who aren't completely immersed in it, it might be tough to understand the differences. I say that because, as a Division One college soccer player, you go from the Autumn season to the Spring season, playing daily for around 6 months straight with a few breaks in between.

Once you've ended your Spring season with your college team, literally the next day you are expected to be competing with your PDL team.

That's why I think you see a lot of guys getting injured in the summer months playing PDL, the work load is just a lot to handle.

In terms of overall quality, I would be foolish to think that the NYRB U23s isn't the most technically gifted team I've ever been on in my life. Not necessarily the best team I've ever been on, but definitely the most talented team, which makes training very competitive and very intense.

I think college football is different because there is much more of a sense of 'working together to achieve a common goal' approach and mind-set whereas with the

New York Red Bulls it's much more of an 'I have to do whatever I can to make sure that I'm invited to first team training next week" mind-set.

Now, that's not at all to say that there was anything wrong with how these guys approached training; I just think it's a different mind-set which is once again harboured by the environment you're put in.

After college, what are your plans going forward?

Hopefully, professional football is up next for me. All I've ever wanted from life since the time I was introduced to football was to play professionally. Approaching the transition from amateur to professional in America is much different than in any other country in the world.

Having coaches that are as connected as Coach McCourt and Hughie are is a great resource to have moving forward. I haven't even played my senior season yet at Monmouth and they've put me in professional environments to be seen by professional coaches which is all any college footballer could ask for.

Following my senior season, each Major League Soccer team has its own little combines that they invite potential draft picks to, before the actual MLS Combine in a couple of months. So, hopefully, I play well enough in the Autumn to get invited to some of those combines to get seen by some of the coaches!

From there, it's all about playing when it matters. I need to perform in those environments in order to interest a club enough to pick me up in the MLS Draft.

The draft is in January so from the end of my season with Monmouth until the draft I'll be working harder than I ever have before. During that span, I'll also probably be choosing an agent to represent me. I think having a good agent is completely necessary if you want to make good choices within your career.

If I don't get drafted or I get injured or anything else that could hinder my chance of being brought into a club happens, then obviously my course of action will be re-evaluated with the help of my coaching staff at Monmouth, TSF and my parents, but for now that's my main route forward...

You're also certainly keeping yourself busy with EKGoalkeeper Training. How did the idea for this come about and how is it going at present?

Starting EKGKT was a no brainer. I love football and goalkeeping and I couldn't imagine doing anything other than coaching in my life after football is over. Last summer, I got invited to the NCAA 'Career in Sports' forum.

The NCAA, for those who don't know, is the governing body of collegiate sports. The 'Career in Sports' forum is a prestigious event hosted by the NCAA at their headquarters in Indianapolis for four days in July every year.

The forum is meant to prepare student-athletes for life after college and figure out what they want to do. It is geared towards those who want to go into working within the NCAA in some capacity.

Essentially, it's a big network of athletes and college coaches that's done every year to teach student-athletes how to become college coaches. When I attended this event it became clear that all I wanted to was to coach.

I met some very influential people and was impacted a lot by their knowledge, their character and their stories of life as a collegiate coach. After this point, I knew that I needed to start taking my coaching seriously, so I started coaching more.

Coaching young goalkeepers and teaching them the nature of goalkeeping and of life in general is something I live for.

Starting EKGKT is just a part of the process of becoming a high-level coach. Since EKGKT's inception it's gone amazingly well: I've worked with some really great people, made some good connections, really impacted some amazing young footballers and I couldn't be happier with the way my life is unfolding to be honest.

How does the pathway system for American goalkeepers look?

I think one of the most important things to remember when talking about the United States footballing system is that it is

constantly fluctuating and still in search of a real identity in a lot of ways. However, I don't think it's really any different for a goalkeeper than for a field player.

Currently, the United States Development Academy is the best league in the country for youth development and it is where the best players are and the best clubs are.

This was not the case when I began playing football. When I started playing football, the US Development Academy didn't exist. I played club football for my entire youth career, which means I didn't play for a massive youth club like a New York Red Bulls Academy or an FC Dallas Academy.

I played for a club which began operations in 2005 and stuck with them from U11 to U23s. The academy system does not allow for players to play for their high schools, which essentially means that high school soccer is dead in terms of finding any real talent, which is a sad but true realisation, especially for someone who takes a lot of pride in representing their high school.

Beyond this, what sort of level of goalkeeper coaching is available to coaches?

Goalkeeper coaching is almost always readily available at Division One universities. I only know of a handful of schools across the 200 plus Division One schools which don't have full-time goalkeeper coaches.

In terms of high school goalkeeper coaching, high school soccer isn't very serious anymore or valuable to be honest so that isn't exactly relevant. Academies, on the other hand, have multiple goalkeeper coaches.

My club, TSF Academy isn't one of the biggest clubs in the country but it's fairly big in terms of the state and the region and we have at least three to four academy goalkeeper coaches at any given time.

How far do you think the facilities go to developing elite American talent?

I think the facilities at Monmouth and most universities are very good. The NCAA has requirements that are structured and very organised, which allows us to play at pretty good facilities for most of the season and off-season.

In terms of playing in front of big crowds, I think it's quite similar to the UK. Our universities might be the ones pulling crowds, where they wouldn't in the UK, but the U18s and U21s of the really big clubs in England pull just as big crowds as most universities I would say.

Freshman year at college most players are 18 years old so, in the UK, you would be at the point where it's time to either sign a professional contract or hang it up... There's definitely some overlap.

You can find out more about Eric Klenofsky's goalkeeper camps via his Twitter @ericklenofsky **and his dedicated Instagram profile** @ekgoalkeepertraining.

A HAT-TRICK OF DEBUTS

WAYNE BROWN

Oxford United First Team Goalkeeper Coach and all-round goalkeeping enthusiast Wayne Brown has got to know many goalkeepers, coaches and fans over the years, but his stories of debuts are maybe the only ones that satisfy both criteria of being both appropriate to this publication and yet a fascinating insight into the goalkeeper union!

BRISTOL CITY

At the age of 16, I was playing for the non-league side Bashley Town when I got wind that Bristol were coming down to have a look at me. To cut a long story short, they ended up buying me for £40,000 (not bad for a 16-year-old!) and I was thrown straight in at the deep end...

For my debut, I remember that we played Peterborough at home and it was the last game of the season, so there was nothing really riding on it. As usual, I was doing the normal match day jobs that the scholars would do, such as preparing the kit rooms and cleaning boots and next thing I know I'm playing for the first team!

I was only actually told that I would be playing at about 12:15PM, after having played a youth team game that morning, in fact. The manager at the time called me in (and there I was thinking that I was in trouble after we'd lost our earlier game!) and he basically told me that I was going to play to be playing that afternoon. Shocked probably doesn't quite do it justice.

It was incredible,really, considering I was going to be up against two Peterborough strikers who were 6"4 tall and in front of a 9,000 crowd...

If I'm going to be honest with you, I've got no recollection of the game or how I did. I must have played well, though, because I got man of the match and did make a few decent saves, too, according to the highlights video!

OXFORD UNITED

I actually moved to Oxford with the view of being a backup goalkeeper and then, over time, developing into the coaching role as well. My debut, however, did not quite go as planned...

It was against Southend United at The Kassam Stadium, in a cup match, I believe, and my Dad had come down to watch it. About 10 minutes in, a ball came over the top and, as soon as it bounced, I knew that it had me.

There was just that moment, that realisation, as a goalkeeper when you know that you've got this one wrong and can foresee the oncoming carnage.

I'd come rushing out and maybe got my decisions a little bit wrong, before ending up handballing the ball, giving away a free-kick and getting myself sent off in the process! Not a great start for your debut, or all 12 minutes of it anyway...

Another outfield lad, Asa Hall, then went in goal and conceded the ensuing free-kick by standing behind the wall!

The worst part about it was, though, that my Dad who had come down to watch the game on his motorbike was about 15 minutes late...

By the time he got to the ground, I'd already been sent off so he didn't get to see me play at all. I probably shouldn't tell you what he said to me in the bar afterwards....!

SOUTH AFRICA

During my career, as well, I spent a brief bit of time playing for SuperSport United in South Africa. It was an incredible experience for a variety of reasons and my debut was one of those occasions that really stood out.

I remember for my debut, though, I'd only got off the plane two days before and was absolutely exhausted.

On the way to the match, we got to the coach and all of a sudden the players started to sing. From the hotel to the stadium and then into the changing rooms, the players would always sing all of their tribal songs, I was told, and it was pretty incredible to hear.

I was just sat there as the Englishman who had no idea really what was going on! I remember phoning my girlfriend at the time, telling her to put me on speaker and just saying *"have a listen to this!!"*, as the raucous chants echoed through the coach.

Moving forward to the game, and you must remember that corruption in South Africa is absolutely rife. Probably the most shocking thing about the game was the whole penalty saga: I thought I'd saved two penalties that game, but it would appear the referee thought otherwise...

The first, I dived down to my right and made the save, before the referee turned around and tried to tell me that I moved off my line. I knew full well that I hadn't, but I got up and set myself up for the retake. Once more, same place, I dived and saved it in the bottom right. I couldn't believe it when the referee blew his whistle and pointed to the spot again. I was just thinking, *"What is going on here?! It's ridiculous..."*.

I conceded the third penalty - a different lad who just drove it through me - but I was absolutely raging at the time.

If we then fastforward a bit, there were times in the game when I had the ball in my hand, with the 18-yard line 4 or 5 yards ahead of me and the referee would blow up for a free-kick, as in trying to say I'd handballed it.

It was just all a joke, really.

After the game, when my manager was having a bit of a dig at the officials, I went up to the referee to shake is hand (it's only football at the end of the day!) and he just turns back to me and goes *"Welcome to Africa..."*.

What an experience that was, I had my work cut out over there from the minute go.

FROM SHRIMPS TO DRAGONS...

RICHARD LEE

From coaching networks to healthy coffee, there are few ventures that serial entrepreneur and former Premier League goalkeeper Richard Lee hasn't been involved in. He also owns the worldwide GK Icon franchise, as well as running and coordinating a player management firm, a link to which can be found in Rich's second feature. Famously, though, he appeared on Dragon's Den back in the 2000's:

What was Dragon's Den like as an experience?

Going on Dragon's Den was an incredible experience. It was thanks to my friend who managed to put through the application and was very positive about our project and chances. The very interesting thing about that was that I had to ask Mark Hughes, my new Blackburn manager at the time, if I could go on the show!

I remember the show was being filmed on a Wednesday, but I was not certain at this point that I'd get the day off...

So I knocked on the door and said *"Look, I've been accepted on to a TV show..."*. At first, he was very unsure. It wasn't until I explained to him that it was Dragon's Den that he became very excited – turns out he was a huge fan of the show and wished me luck, telling me to come back and let him know how I got on! The other interesting thing about that was the fact that I had a game in Morecambe the night before. This meant a trip down to London, arriving at around 4AM, before having to be up again at 5AM for the recording, so all of 1 hour of sleep!

Why did you originally choose to get into business?

The main reason that I got into business when I was younger was actually as an escape, and not many people know this. I wasn't particularly enjoying my football at the time but I knew that I couldn't quit because of the financial benefits that it would bring.

There are huge pressures around football and playing in front of such large crowds and I hated the idea that my career could be finished by one injury.

Looking back on it, it was the best decision that I ever made, having now run a number of successful businesses and with the passion that I get for business, so it's a little strange to think it was originally a product of fear!

You can find out more about Rich's business, projects and past successes at www.dickielee.com

FACT FILE: RICHARD LEE

DOB: 5.10.1982

NATIONALITY: ENGLISH

HEIGHT: 6FT (1.83M)

TOTAL APPS: 158

CLUB: RETIRED

INT'L: 2 CAPS FOR ENG U20

BUSINESSES: GK ICON + OTHERS

Starting his career at local team Bedgrove Dynamoes during his childhood years, Rich's career spanned clubs such as Watford, Brentford and Fulham, with appearances mainly concentrated in the Championship, as well as a few in the Premier League, too.

In addition to cameo appearances on TV shows such as Channel 4's 'Come Dine With Me', Rich's current endeavours are heavily revolved around the world of business.

Since retiring at the end of the 2014/15 season, he has put the majority of his time into his Organo Gold coffee campaign and the aforementioned GK Icon, which is now running across multiple continents and in an abundance of different countries, with goalkeepers from all over the world benefitting from the knowledge, experience and coaching excellence of Rich and his dedicated team.

He also wrote the best-selling book 'Graduations, Life Lessons of a Professional Footballer', which is available on various platforms for purchase, as well as attaining a first class honours degree in Media and Journalism, often reporting on the likes of Soccer Saturday.

As if that wasn't enough to be involved in, he also does regular work as a pundit across a variety of TV and radio channels and has a couple more projects lined up for the coming months...

A DANISH AGENDA...

CASPER ANKERGREN

Growing up with idols such as the beast that was Peter Schmeichel, we speak to Brighton and Hove Albion goalkeeper and coach Casper Ankergren all about the rigours of Danish football, what his early footballing life was like and where he hopes his career will take him from now.

Tell us a little more about your background in football, if possible... When did you first get into the game?

I started playing football out on pitch when I was around 8 years old but I couldn't concentrate at all. I was just sitting on the grass looking at worms most of the time...

I also remember one funny time when I thought I had scored a goal but then realised it was in the wrong net; I was really struggling there!!

I didn't start playing in goal until quite late on in my development - I think I was about 13 at the time. I used to play every position on the pitch, which benefitted me hugely later on.

As I moved through the years, I ended up playing semi-pro, working in a pizzeria, kindergarten and at an afterschool club all at the same time...

I was offered my first professional contract in May 2000, when Brøndby IF bought me from Køge, and that was where my football career really began to take off.

Obviously you came up, as well, through the Danish footballing system. How does goalkeeping over there compare to how we see it in the UK?

I didn't have a specialist goalkeeper coach until I was about 17. I just joined in in whatever the outfield players were doing and then went in goal when we were playing 8v8 or doing a shooting drill.

I would have benefitted massively from having a goalkeeper coach, but then again I learned a lot from joining in as an outfield player. My first goalkeeper coach was from Yugoslavia and I learnt an awful lot from him...

It was very different from what we do today but I could really feel the benefit – especially as I had come from virtually no coaching at all.

My technique got a lot better from just having a coach once a week for an hour (I was still only semi-pro and trained about 3 times a week) and so I am very thankful for that.

It wasn't until I signed for Brøndby that I was working with a goalkeeper coach every day. It was a completely new world to me and a totally different level; it took me a long time to get used to it.

Jørgen Henriksen was my coach at the time. He used to work with Peter Schmeichel when he was at Brøndby and he also did the national team.

He was a bit old school but a great guy who taught me a lot about being a goalkeeper and a person. I still keep in touch with him today, in fact.

His sessions weren't too technically orientated. He wasn't bothered whether you took off on your right or left leg when a cross came in or if you could kick with your weak foot. Maybe this is one of the reasons Scmeichel thrived with his own, individual style...

We worked hard and he always reminded us about how lucky we were to have a job like this. I remember, he would specifically say, *"Don't take anything in this life for granted"*.

Did you play any other sports through youth?

Before I signed for Brøndby, I used to play handball during the winter break. I wasn't too bad at it, actually... I ended up getting called up for the national team!

I had to turn it down, though, as my parents were worried it was going to be too much

for me with my footballing commitment, too, which was probably the correct decision.

They said I had to choose between football and handball but that they would support me in whatever I wanted to do. It was easy for me to pick football as handball was just something I was doing when there was a break from football.

I definitely think that I've taken some things from playing in goal with handball into football... Not being afraid of getting a ball smashed in your face (it still hurts though!!) and coming out of your goal and making yourself as big as possible are two great examples.

How does the standard of the Danish top-league compare to England for goalkeeping?

The Danish League is very technical in that most teams try and play football. We used to play out from the back, especially when Michael Laudrup took over... He really wanted us to play entertaining football.

My time in Leeds was a bit different, to say the least! I wasn't allowed to pass it to my centre-backs under Dennis Wise. It was more or less route one.

Things changed under other managers and, in spite of the different football, I had a really good time at Leeds. In Brøndby, the fans were great and were behind the team 99% of time no matter what the result.

At Leeds, on the other hand, the fans were mad! I remember how excited they would get from just getting a corner and I loved it. It seemed like the whole city was interested in Leeds United.

I fell in love with English football straight away.

My loan spell went well, personally, but – as a team - we ended up getting relegated to League One. It wasn't a nice experience. The club had to get let go a lot of good people and we went under administration.

I stuck with the club, though, and had a fantastic season the following year. We would have got promoted if we hadn't started the campaign on minus 15 points. Still, we went all the way to the playoff final, losing 1-0 to Doncaster.

My second year was an awful lot of being in and out of the team but we ended up getting beaten in the playoff semi-final against Millwall.

In my third year, we finally got promoted and I think I played about 30 games... Simon Grayson, though, was the manager and he didn't really like me which is fair enough.

I then moved to Brighton where Gus Poyet was in charge. I knew Gus from Leeds, where he was the assistant manager under Dennis. Gus made it clear that we would be playing total football...

He would go mad at me if I played it long and I could have passed it out! We had a great year, winning League One that season, which was 2010-11 I believe.

We didn't have the best players in the league but we had an incredible team spirit and everybody understood their roles so we played really good entertaining football. What made it even better was that the season after the Amex was ready, which is a fantastic stadium, and I am thoroughly

enjoying the game time I get here! The following season, I played half of the games and we finished mid-table in the Championship.

Then, Tomasz came to the club and since then I've really only played a handful of games each season.

I'm third choice goalkeeper at the moment, which wasn't easy to accept in the beginning, but after getting my head around it it's ok – I'm 37 now and understand my role, which is moving more and more towards the coaching perspective.

I am more than happy to coach whenever I am needed and, hopefully, this year I will get my own age group and take them twice a week in the evenings.

I really appreciate what this football club has done for me over the years and long may it continue!

What current coaching do you do, how did you get into it and why did you think it was for you?

Football is my life. I can't imagine not continuing working in and around football.

I've always loved training and always knew that coaching was the way that I wanted to go when I retired from playing.

I've done my FA Outfield Level 2 and this summer I've just finished my UEFA B outfield up at West Ham's academy training ground, which I have to take as otherwise I wouldn't be allowed to do my UEFA B goalkeeper badges.

Moving forward a bit, I then went up to St Georges Park for a week to do my UEFA B goalkeeper course, which I really enjoyed.

Now I just need to do a lot of coaching back in Brighton and then I will have my final assessment in both badges at the end of the year if all goes according to plan!

FROM SKIING TO COACHING

JON HORTON

From school football to Alpine skiing and then back Into the world of coaching, there isn't much that Wales Women's Goalkeeper Coach Jon Horton hasn't come across in his time. Inspired by the likes of Peter Shilton, Jon started off as a coach of his child's Sunday League team, before his qualifications took him much further and deeper into the world of sport…

How did you initially get into goalkeeper coaching?

My background is an unusual one but one heavily-based around sport participation and sports coaching within that. At school, I loved PE and attained a reasonable level at most sports. Despite the fact I am by no means the tallest, I found myself in goal as I loved to throw myself around and end up face first in the mud!

I was a season ticket holder at Southampton FC throughout the 80's and was inspired by the story and talent of Peter Shilton. When Peter joined Southampton in 1982, I was lucky enough to get to know him and his family as they lived in the next road up from mine.

Our families became close and I was able to see in detail and personally the dedication, desire and talent he possessed.

Despite this, and the attractions of football, my head was turned when I learnt to ski and got involved in Alpine Ski Racing.

I competed in the Slalom & Giant Slalom up to National Squad level and, after finishing competing at 18, I pursued a career in skiing coaching, working through my badges to the point where I was actually at a National Coaching level.

My enjoyment of goalkeeping did not fade through this time and, at any opportunity, I would get between the posts for a Sunday League side or a friendly kickabout!

Things changed when I got married and had children… 3 boys in total!

When the eldest turned 8 years old and asked to play for the local club, I stepped forward to help coach the side and began the process of gaining qualifications at the ripe old age of 37.

My boys then became involved with Reading FC Elite Centre and so I applied to become a coach within the system and continued my qualifications to include the goalkeeping levels and further.

A colleague within the club was the goalkeeper for the Women's Team at Reading FC at the time, which had recently achieved

FA WSL 2 status, and said they were looking for a Reserve Team GK Coach.

I went along and met Kelly Chambers and the Arsenal and Wales legend that is Jayne Ludlow, who had recently been appointed Manager of Reading Women's FC.

After running a few sessions I was offered the role working with both reserve and first team goalkeepers!

My role over the season expanded and I combined my goalkeeper coaching role with others, helping the club work towards promotion to FA WSL 1.

When Jayne Ludlow left RWFC to take on the role of Wales Women's Team Manager, Jayne asked me to help with the goalkeepers in the Wales team in conjunction with my current roles

In early 2016, after helping RWFC to the FA WSL 2 title and promotion to FA WSL 1, I was offered a more permanent role with the Wales Women's Teams and Jayne Ludlow, which provided me with a better work life balance and I now head-up the programme for U17, U19's and Senior Women at FA Wales.

Do you see many differences between the male and female game?

I wouldn't really say that there are any profound differences between the two at all, really.

With all the women and girls I work with, I look to focus on the basic understanding and mechanics of efficient footwork and sound handling as the fundamentals.

If the mechanics behind these are instilled in a goalkeeper and become the norm with them, then anything else is possible with the help and support of strength and conditioning coaches, which I suppose play a different role to that with males.

I understand the differences physically and psychologically working with females but this does not mean a female cannot pull off a top-corner save like her male counterpart and that's what I strive to do with all the goalkeepers I work with.

In honesty, every female goalkeeper I have worked with is different: they all have strengths and weaknesses that encompass all aspects of goalkeeping!

In sport overall, though, my experience working with female skiers and goalkeepers is that they apply techniques to a more accurate level when learning than men, very often, and I believe this is to compensate where power and strength is not a natural attribute.

Transitioning slightly, what sort of differences are there in the way you coach female goalkeepers?

The main difference within the women's game, as aforementioned, is the speed and power. Therefore, within sessions we have to adapt the pace of the serving/ball delivery. Workload is monitored and adapted according to the individual but overall is slightly lower than what would be applied to a male counterpart.

Psychologically, they are very different beasts. As they say, men are from Mars and women are from Venus!

During my time in the women's game I have learnt a lot about managing individuals which is especially hard in goalkeeping when you work with 3 or 4 goalkeepers all fighting for the No1 spot.

I have learnt to build individual coaching relationships with each of them and to adapt my coaching style within a practice for each goalkeeper in order to maximise their learning and outcomes.

Moving on to the international picture, how big do you find the contrast is between club goalkeeping in the WSL and that of international teams?

The gap between FA WSL and international football for the goalkeepers themselves is not much different, especially given the standard of football in the FA WSL 1.

As a coach, the environment has its pros and cons with the intensity being more fragmented and the time you have with the goalkeepers considerably limited - you are less able to effect their development.

In Wales, we counter this by liaising with the clubs and giving International Camp reports based on learning, outcomes and areas of development.

This is also combined with weekly training sessions with the Wales coaching staff, where our international department covers U17 and U19 age groups.

This is enabling myself, as a coach, to bridge the gap between club and country for goalkeepers going forwards, meaning a bright future for Welsh goalkeeping hopefully!

Finally, and just to finish off, for coaches that may be beginning to coach in the female world, what would be the advice that you give them?

Definitely start by looking to work with mixed-sex teams in grassroots to support your understanding of the challenges females face within the sport, socially, physically and psychologically (tactically and technically I apply the same demands on my goalkeepers regardless of sex). Spend some time watching the female game so that you see it for what it is...

A sport we love, a national institution and something we want to be involved: football!!

Thereafter, manage your expectations but don't be frightened to challenge females to match their male counterparts because more often than not they are capable of it.

WORKING WITH DISABLED SQUADS

TONY ELLIOTT

For our final feature in the section, Tony Elliott tells us a little bit more about the disabled FA squads, the added challenges in working with them and the rewards for doing so for a coach.

What different disabled squads have you worked with over your period as a coach?

I've worked with the Cerebral Palsy Squad who, incidentally, are going to Rio this summer for the Paralympic games, and also the blind squad, even though the goalkeeper is fully sighted.

How fundamental are the differences between the sports?

I think there is a big difference to be managed. We don't treat the players any differently but there are some challenges that do occur when working with disability squads.

I like to think that I have adapted to these differences and acted accordingly, but we really had to look to put together syllabuses to build up goalkeepers who could work within the constraints of the game.

Some people would say that it's just football, at the end of the day, but then we break

it down and we see that the CP squad play 7-a-side on a grass pitch with slightly smaller goals etc., so it brings about a different game and contexts for the goalkeeper to adapt to, just like futsal or other sports where we prepare differently.

In the different classifaction scales, where does the CP goalkeeper usually fit?

The goalkeeper would normally be classification 5, which means a restriction of movement in the lower limbs and therefore difficulty passing the ball off the ground and distribution in that sense.

Is it more of a challenge working with these athletes?

It's very challenging but massively, massively rewarding at the same time.

I have had the privilege of working with these goalkeepers in the run up to major tournaments and their journey really is phenomenal, with a wonderful opportunity to play in the pinnacle tournament of any disabled sports persons career: the Paralympics.

Hopefully they can show the world how good they are, because we really do have some of the best goalkeepers globally in Great Britain.

THE TALENT PATHWAY

How can we predict, at the age of 7, who is going to become the next Premier League giant? We probably can't, no matter what anyone says, but understanding why this is and the whole multitude of cultural, social and developmental factors that will effect this underpins this section within the book. We look at the likes of Jack Butland and their early phases, whilst also discussing the best way for coaches and academies to grow and nurture their goalkeepers.

MC — Max Crocombe - Oxford United and New Zealand U23 Goalkeeper

DT — Dean Thornton - QPR Lead Academy Goalkeeping Coach and former England Futsal International

NL — Nick Levett - The FA's Talent Identification Manager and holder of a Master's degree in Learning & Creativity

MC — Matt Campbell - Former Manchester United academy product and Blackburn Rovers scholar

OM — Oliver Martin - Non-League Goalkeeper, formerly with Manchester City

NATURE OR NURTURE?

MCR - MCA - DT - NL - OM

Given the fact that most goalkeepers won't reach their peak until moving into their late-20s, the goalkeeping talent pathway has always been a thoroughly interesting one and something that consistently probes discussion, debate and deliberation over the best ways to nurture our young talent. Nick Levett, National Talent ID Manager for The FA shares with us a little bit more:

Is it possible to put together, or reverse engineer, the goalkeeper journey and look at how the goalkeepers have got where they are today?

I'm not sure you can, for a variety of different reasons.

There are so many different factors that come into play: they've got different parents, different home situations, they're getting into sport at different times, they would have played out on the streets depending on where they live...

All of this is going to look totally different depending on the kid. I just don't think there is a 'right way'; every different player that I speak to has a totally different story and, whilst there may be some recurring themes like informal play, the individual differences are so wide I don't really think you can nail it.

In your opinion, when should goalkeepers specialise in just goalkeeping?

Well, we pick the England team from U15 upwards. The laws of the game tell us that we need a goalkeeper, so we need a goalkeeper by U15. Whether they're specialised as a goalkeeper or not is probably a different question.

Certainly, if you look at elite goalkeeper pathways, there will be big differences.

For example, if you look at Jack Butland, he wasn't playing 100% football still at age 15. It was probably about 80%, with the rest made up of a mixture of cricket, rugby and athletics through the years.

In the foundation phase (5-11) it was only 20% football and at 12-14 it still wasn't even 50%.

Of course, there's the chance that he's an outlier but I feel there's a huge amount of benefit to playing different sports that have transferable skills.

For example, if he/she as a goalkeeper are doing sports such as basketball, volleyball, rugby, there's probably some real benefit to

it.

You're doing things like tracking a moving object and working on hand-eye coordination but you've also got to trade off and continue to work on the bits you don't get. Distribution, working on angles, protecting the goal and the more horizontal/lateral nature of goalkeeping compared to the linear nature of basketball, for example, are areas that will still need to be improved.

I think there's a massive amount of benefit in multi-sport, though, so if they're still doing that through their early teenage years then great.

Especially in the development phase, I think that there are also huge benefits to goalkeepers of playing out on pitch.

If the stats are what they are about hand-to-feet ratios, and also the fact that a lot of clubs now have the philosophy of playing out from the back, it's going to be absolutely vital that goalkeepers can play with their feet.

I'd certainly, also, say that kids at the foundation stage should rotate as the goalkeeper. You've got no idea how tall these kids are going to be and where they're going to play 5 or 10 years down the line.

You have no idea if you're big, tall centre-half at the minute, who plays there because he

can lump the ball forward and you think you

can win more matches, will actually be your best long-term goalkeeper. Giving kids that exposure is definitely worth it.

What about an elite goalkeeper's mind-set: do you believe that is something developed or innate?

As a goalkeeper, you definitely need a different mind-set to an outfield player. It's probably developed through a bit of both nature and nurture, but your life experiences will dictate the skills you take to those experiences later in life.

So, if you've never had to deal with failure at any point in your life, by the time you get to it – at least at the high-performance end – you're going to struggle because you haven't got the skills to deal with it.

Everyone will have these negative experiences, and you can't protect people from the times, but it's imperative that you've got people around you to support you at these points and at certain times maybe you need to manufacture those negatives to deliberately mess people up and force them to find a solution.

For example, there's one player who's an

England U21. He's always been physically ahead so played a year above in the academies and really never failed anything in his life.

He's only starting to fail now that he's going out on loan. And this will be the making or breaking of his entire career: has he got the skills with it now to deal with it when the going gets tough?

I think that we definitely need to be brave enough to push players into this situation where they're going to experience stress, trauma and difficulty so that they then acquire the skills to deal with it.

However, you can't just drop them into a hole and hope that they survive: you need to make sure you've got the right support network in there too.

There's a story, actually, about a high-flying youth team player. The coaching squad dropped him from an FA Cup Youth game. It was a huge game for the kids and this was a League Two club.

The reason they did it was not performance-related but instead for the long-term benefit for that kid in dealing with a setback. How are you going to deal with it?

I think sometimes we're not brave enough to do that because we're worrying about our own ego and the score of that game as oppose to the long-term outcome for the kid.

THE PATHWAY IN PROGRESS...

MCR - MCA - DT - NL - OM

Oxford United and New Zealand goalkeeper Max Crocombe grew up through the MK Dons academy. When he found himself back playing Sunday League football at the age of 16, though, he knew something had to change and so set himself out to get in front of a professional club. A perfect example of a footballer just at the beginning of his professional pathway, there is plenty more in store for the young international, with getting game time the foremost concern:

How did you make the change from playing mid-week football and doing A-Levels to getting your scholar deal?

I actually got into Oxford United initially through an email that I sent to them... I got through my first year of A-Levels and had an absolutely manic schedule – probably testament to my love of football!

I was playing three games in a weekend, before having a rest day on Monday and Friday, training on a Thursday and extra matches on a Tuesday and Wednesday (including time upfront on a Wednesday!)...

It was just games, games, games, and then I was playing and managing the school team as well.

It was when I was just starting my second year of A-Levels, having been told that I had teams watching me, that I just decided I had to be playing football. I got into the county team for Berks and Bucks at the same time, and this really made me confident to move things forward to the next club.

I shot off an email to Les Taylor at Oxford United, as well as a couple of other clubs, then went down there for a two-week trial and the next thing I know I've signed up...

I actually signed as a two-year scholar, which meant it took me through to my third year of further education. It was an incredible experience looking back, though, and a huge eye opener. Just going in from the nice, comfortable environment of school to the world of football, where it's such a tough apprenticeship, was really difficult.

Not just from a mental perspective, but physically, also, as I was doing several sessions with the goalkeepers, the youth team and the first team all mixed in together. Everything was so new to me and I absolutely loved it. I injured my shoulder through the middle of my scholar, which was a bit of a nightmare, but I came back from it and had another 6 months before Chris Wilder gave me my first professional contract.

Moving forward, obviously I had a couple of successful loan spells last year which were really interesting experiences, but for me now it's just all about playing football.

You went on loan to Southport and Nuneaton Town last season, what were these experiences like?

I'd say it was very hard, but I really liked it. I thrive on positions where you're up against it and you're being tested. Sure: I like to be confident and comfortable in my environment, but always so that there's just that little bit of edge and something to play for.

Nevertheless, at the end of the day and however you spin it, going into the bottom of the conference is tough, especially where every point is important - a bit of a different approach to the youth team games.

Mistakes in the youth team are all hypothetical, whereas in these games there's no holding back and people make it clear that dropping your standards isn't good enough.

I think that it's vital for young players, you just have to take the criticism, experience and any mistakes that come with it on the chin and move on. It's just a situation where these guys really want to win and – from

my experience so far – I've not seen any criticism in a dressing room that I'd consider a personal attack, it's an emotional game and people will speak their mind.

How do you deal with the insults from the crowd at non-league level?

I take it as a compliment more than anything. I'm a fan myself and, when I'm in the stands, you're envious of the other good players – those are the ones you try and boo. The other reason they're doing it, of course, is simply because you're the closest to them. Normally, if their team isn't winning, you'd expect to have played some part in that as a goalkeeper so you can start to understand why they're having a pop at you.

The pressure is there and I enjoy it, no doubt. At some point in your career you're going to receive criticism. Hopefully it doesn't happen too often to you but there's no way anyone can have a spotless career.

What would your advice be to a young, 15-year-old goalkeeper looking to take things a step forward?

Listen to everyone, certainly. But always keep the mental strength to be able to block out people's opinions.

There's always going to be someone criticising you unless you're supremely talented, regardless of where you are in your career.

Joe Hart is a perfect example. He's one of the best goalkeepers in my lifetime and arguably one of the best to ever come out of England and yet he's picked up a lot of stick from the Euros 2016, which is a bit harsh in my eyes, but it shows you that people are always ready to level their opinions.

Definitely, the biggest thing is to enjoy the pressure, believe in yourself and enjoy the feeling of stopping the ball going into your net. So many people get frustrated and disappointed by it, but never lose your belief at the end of the day.

What about in training, what approach do you take there?

From a training perspective, I think it's important to build a solid base for yourself in terms of techniques and working habits. It's vital to keep working on it so that it becomes consistent, reliable and what works for you.

Enjoying the hard work that comes with the training and practising certainly makes it easier. From there, you start trying out different techniques in certain situations that you've seen other goalkeepers doing but at the same time it's important not to be over-consumed by it. There's so much information out there ...

For me, that's what training is for: don't necessarily get caught up with training in one way, just practice it as you find feels right to you.

If you look at all the top goalkeepers, they don't use textbook techniques – they don't perform exactly how you would coach them to do something. I think, as a goalkeeper, it's all about understanding this and working out what works best for you.

What advice would you give for getting yourself out there?

The biggest thing I'd say is that you need to just be playing and enjoying it. One of the best things that happened to me when I was released was that I could keep playing.

I sort of fell out of love with football for a little while but then, when I was able to go back to Sunday League, I really started to enjoy my football again because I could just relax and enjoy it. I'm playing football on the Sunday and going back to school on the Monday and we could just chat about and relive the game - it's all a hobby again.

I was just recreating my positive state without even knowing or realising it. I do that these days when I'm struggling as a professional, too. There are times when the game can get on top of you but I would take this as a trigger to visit that positive state, when playing with my mates, that very much helps me return to where I play at my best.

How do you try and get yourself through the difficult patches?

Things might not happen as you want them to and there are times when you will make mistakes. However, the only way to move on from them is to analyse them honestly - I generally do it the next day once the emotions of the game have settled, correcting why things went wrong.

I keep my belief through the difficult times because a former team-mate of mine used to say *"you have to believe in yourself because nobody else is going to do it for you"* and it's stuck with me.

If I'm honest, my best development has been when I've taken the lead and not waited for a coach (no matter how great they may be) to make the movements for me. There's a saying *"when the student's ready, the teacher will appear"*bv. Certainly, you need to be ready and motivated in yourself if you want to learn.

What is your plan now moving forwards?

Nowadays, I don't actually think I have a specific plan. When I was in the youth team, I

had a particular pathway, moving from there to get into the first team at Oxford United and New Zealand.

My thing at the moment, though, is literally just about playing... I've had conversations with the gaffer to see if I could get some game time because I was really determined to go out and get some match experience on my CV.

We both agreed that it was probably best for me to get some games and I believe that quite often you do have to make the first move about these decisions, as oppose to just passively waiting in the comfort of where you are at the present.

So yes, certainly, the number one aim now is to be playing competitive football.

THE GAME OF TALENT ID

MCR - MCA - DT - NL - OM

It's a cold, wet January morning. The idea of the grey-haired silhouette in a long, black puffer jacket, frivolously scribbling down notes onto a cork clipboard may be slightly past us now, but that doesn't mean the world of Talent Identification (or 'Talent ID' as it's more commonly known amongst the right kind of circles) is any less fiercely contested, as a host of professionals try to explain exactly why their philosophy is the best for recognising and inspiring young talent... Nick Levett shares his opinions once more:

When scouts go out there looking for goalkeepers, what sort of specification are they working to?

It will vary from club to club. And beyond this from individual to individual. The club will have a footballing philosophy on paper, but an individual scout may well interpret this very differently.

If your first team manager says the goalkeeper has to be 6"3 with these technical/tactical attributes, then that's what the scouting department will find.

I think in the foundation phase, though, without having that long-term information of what you're going to get out of the player, some coaches will still look for the goalkeeper who wants to play in goal.

Many are often pushed into it by a very keen mum or dad who sees their child as the next Joe Hart because "*I failed my career so this is what you're going to achieve*", although that is getting much better – there's only a little bit of that around these days.

For me, it should still be that you just love playing football and happen to be quite good at it.

I worked at a club where they recruited goalkeepers, from grassroots, that would become the foundation phase goalkeeper.

In my opinion, yes – these goalkeepers should still be playing in goal. However, maybe this is just for period 1 and 2 during one game and 3 and 4 the next, maybe playing outfield for some of the rest of the time. But I think that if the kid has a genuine desire to play in goal, that's important too and we should respect that.

I've never met a goalkeeper who's not quirky in their own way, too, and if they're brave enough to throw themselves around on a cold December morning then great, but we're talking about a situation here where they may not peak as a goalkeeper until they're 27, 28, 29 and I'm talking about working with a kid who's 20 years younger than that!

From the whole 6 years that I was at a BPL academy, of all the different goalkeepers that I saw, maybe one person who was a goalkeeper at U10 is still a goalkeeper there now. One kid who played out on pitch for U9s/10s, who was struggling as an outfield player so I played him in goal, he's been in the England U15 development squad recently as a goalkeeper. I don't take any credit for that because he's done all the work but it's understanding how that primary position can change over time.

I mean, some coaches – of course – will know where players will be best and whether they'll make it as a professional because they're wizards and they can predict the future!

Most of the time it's just about trying different dynamics at this stage and seeing what works.

Why do these foundation phase goalkeepers often drop out?

I think it's probably a mixture of maybe not being up to the standard and also deciding that, actually, they don't want to play in goal.

Possibly, also, because once you've got through this growth and maturation phase, you've got a better idea of what will be coming out the other side and you'll have more of these late developing goalkeepers that will naturally push the others out, or at least dilute these numbers.

How do you see the importance of height in goalkeeping?

I think that long-term this depends on the philosophy of the manager. If, for whatever reason, they want a goalkeeper that is 6"3 then fine - that is their individual philosophy and you have to work with that.

My argument would probably be look at somebody like Iker Casillas: 5"11. Yet he's still pretty much won everything in world football.

We definitely have to consider standing jump equally to height as well... Would you rather have a goalkeeper who is 6"5 with an 8 inch standing jump or a goalkeeper who is 5"7 with a 40 inch standing jump? I think I know who I'd rather have.

So I think that height can be a little of a misdirecting measurement. For example, one of our goalkeeping scouts once said to me "the difference between 6"1 and 6"3 is the size of a Cadburys Crème Egg", and you have to consider how much that actually matters.

Another interesting facet is the science of the 'Ape Index', which is this really strange idea that, genetically, the way that we're made, a person's wingspan is also their height, in the same way your forearm is the length of your foot.

However, there are certain people who just don't seem to fit that. For example, Michael Phelps, the swimmer, just doesn't conform to the Ape Index – he's somewhat of a freak of nature.

So, if you've got someone who has a wingspan which is 2 or 3 inches longer than their height, that is probably likely to make a big difference too.

This is definitely something to consider for scouts and coaches, as well as the sports science teams!

What about coaches who predict or gamble on the height of goalkeepers?

Gambling on a 9-year-old, telling them they're not going to be 6", is a gamble. But do they do it? Absolutely. With the classic of, *"Look at his mum and dad's height"*. Well, as a starter, how do you know that's his real dad?!
Evolution is telling us that we're getting taller as human beings and, therefore, to say that mum is that big and therefore son or daughter will only be this big is a gamble once more, as well as compounded by the fact that sometimes genetically it skips generations.

I know one kid who had a mum that was about 5"1, but his dad was over 6"... How tall was he going to be? I'm sure there are some sports scientists that plot the height as far as peak-height velocity and when they're going to hit growth spurts etc., with x-rays to the wrist and that's absolutely fine, but I think that it really needs to go back anyway to much broader aspects than just height.

With academy goalkeeping at the moment, what changes do we need to see happen in order to further progress the development of goalkeepers?

I think that we need to be more patient than we are, certainly as they hit puberty in that teenage year group. It's a crucial time for the goalkeepers and their development but we've got no idea what is going to come out the other side.

Especially when they hit that maturation phase, there are going to be all sorts of changes technically and tactically that they're going to be exposed to: look at that goalkeeper who, previously, was great at playing out from the back and all of a sudden the accuracy of their distribution is no longer what it was because they've grown an inch in a week and their body proportions are no longer the same!

We need to recognise that that will happen. Kids in these age groups will make mistakes and you're not going to get consistent performances week-in-week-out.

Take John Stones, for example, who played down an age group during his academy years because of how late he was in developing. Barnsley, though, were patient with him and recognised that he could play technically and look at where he is now.

The same applies to goalkeeping: don't make a snap decision on one physical component, take a picture of the whole situation and look at things from there, would be my message to coaches and academy coaches.

REALITY OF THE DREAM...

MCR - MCA - DT - NL - OM

A young 10-year-old when he first picked up the gloves, it would only take a couple of years for Oliver Martin to be the name hot on the lips of a multitude of scouts across the North, from Bolton Wanderers to Liverpool.

Eventually signing for Manchester City as a school boy, Oliver's career was an abundance of ups and downs, from senior team call-ups to conceding 5, with a red card to top it all off in the realms of non-league...

Tell us a little about your journey: where did it all begin?

As with most young goalkeepers' careers, it started with being the tallest in my year and so I thought I'd give it a shot between the sticks!

It was my final year in primary school, and I decided to try out for the football team. From this came an undefeated season as captain, along with the Footballer of the Year award to top it off...

During my first year of football, I joined the local Sunday league team – Stockport Junior Blues - where I spent just under 3 years before moving to league rivals Reddish Vulcans.

It was here where I grew in confidence, as I was loved and appreciated at the club, albeit I was only there for the one season!

It was this very season in which I began to realise that I could potentially have a chance to make something of a career from the game, with numerous professional clubs including the likes of Bolton Wanderers, Manchester United, Liverpool and finally Manchester City (who I eventually signed for) all expressing their interest in me.

It was here, at Manchester City, that I began to learn the seriousness of football and how important it is to progress yourself as much as possible.

Moving into this, what sort of differences in the commitment were there when you made this step into the academy world?

We were taken out of school two days a week to train, with mainly games against the other Premier League teams coming on a Saturday.

As the years passed by, the competition got stronger and stronger, especially with the new ownership of the club which attracted international standard players.

This would eventually be the reason for my release at 16, as the coaches didn't see me as an international goalkeeper. I suppose matters weren't helped when the England International Angus Gunn was brought in, and I don't think Italy were too short on goalkeepers (family heritage far down the line could have helped me out!).

Gutting, surely... But how did you move forward from here?

It was from here that Fleetwood Town offered me the chance to join their club on a 2-year youth scholarship. During this time, I made huge decisions in my life, through lifestyle choices, becoming more independent, and learning to deal with the consequences of my decisions.

Fleetwood Town progressed me, as I was constantly involved around the first team, joining in with training, warming up on the majority of match days (with a few away games thrown in there) and eventually being named on the bench, too.

I felt that I had done enough to earn a professional contract, especially seen as though I had been putting in consistent performances for both youth and reserve teams, I was youth team captain, had been around the first team for the majority of my scholarship, and there was an U21s team being formed the year after.

Of course, football is a game of opinions, and I obviously didn't fit the bill!

Most people would have probably chucked the towel in at this point... What did you do to stay in the game?

Many of my friends who were released have just left playing professionally alone after that.

However, I was determined to carry on pursuing my goal of playing at the highest level possible. My hopes were met by signing for Conference North outfit Stalybridge Celtic, which was almost perfect for me...

Full time football, a small wage, and constant training.

What wasn't perfect, however, was the fact that I was the No2 goalkeeper for the majority of the season, leaving me without practice and not forwarding my skills.

I cannot stress enough how important it is that, no matter where you are, what club you're at, you must be playing games.

Get game time under your belt. There is only so far that training can take you. Fact.

You then moved on to a brief stint in Sweden, tell us a little more about how that was...

Now, at this time, I had only played 2 games for Stalybridge Celtic, with my debut being cut short after conceding 5 in the first half and then, 2 minutes into the second, getting sent off!

Just when you thought luck couldn't be less on my side, our RB put the gloves on and saved the resulting penalty. I think it's safe to say, no-one asked me for the lottery numbers that night!!

After my 'Stalybridge Shocker' (as it is now known), a couple of new goalkeepers came in and I felt my time was up. I wasn't getting paid much there, I was working for Sports Direct on a shocking wage... I needed a change of scenery. And what better place to do that than Sweden!

The opportunity came about through the League Football Education (LFE), as they had looked after all the scholars during their YT years. Simon Williams got in touch, and simply explained that Ange IF had requested my services.

Around March 2015, I signed for Division 2 Norrland outfit Ange IF in Sweden; time for 3 months of hard work, constant training and relaxation!

Albeit, once again, I only played a couple of games (there seemed to be a pattern

occurring here...) but the experience was one I would never forget. Although I am now back in England, I would gladly snatch at the chance to go back out!

Ange IF gave me the chance to become more independent and concentrate on nothing but my football. 3 months in a foreign country, moving away from all my friends and family, really helped me to grow as an individual and I would love to go back at any time.

I can't thank the LFE enough for introducing me to this, and I strongly feel and would advise that any young player who has been released from a club should sign up for the Erasmus+ programme.

Not only does it give you a new experience, but, in my eyes, it shows other managers that you are prepared to do what it takes to progress your football career.

My point above can be backed up with the fact that I had numerous phone calls with different managers, asking about my services for the season, before I signed for New Mills FC and ended up winning all 4 Player of the Year awards!

Still at the young age of 20, there's plenty of potential for you to continue working up the footballing ladder... Where do you hope to go in the future?

Of course, it is every footballers goal to play as high as possible. I am not only setting my own standards to get back in, but also backing and fully believing in myself that I will, one day, be back at the higher levels.

A well-known advantage of a goalkeeper is that we can play on until we're in our late 30's, so I have the reassurance that I have plenty of time on my hands.

In order to help progress this, I have applied to the V9 Academy, a football academy set up by Jamie Vardy, to highlight some of the players who are good enough to be in the top tiers of the football pyramid but maybe have slipped through the net previously.

With any luck, I will be accepted into this placement and hopefully progress from there!

This trial is exactly the sort of thing I have been waiting for over the last couple of years, so fingers crossed it's something that can work for me!

Finally, looking back, is there anything in particular that you regret about the way your early career panned out?

I definitely have one or two regrets from my young career so far. The main one being back at Manchester City.

At school, I was like any young footballer: I had a passion for sport and competing across the board. With this, I played multiple sports for school such as badminton, track & field and basketball.

I thought I was fitter than what I was and this led to me being tired on game day, maybe not giving the best performances that I could.

I even went to the extent of playing basketball outside of school, on a Friday night and then playing professional academy football with Man City the next day!

What a stupid idea that turned out to be, as I got more injuries from that than I have actually football-related over the years.

It is only when I look back at it now and see my former teammates who have gone on to earn their professional contracts (huge congratulations to all!) playing in the likes of the Youth Champions League, gaining all the boot and glove sponsorship deals, picking up a tidy wage packet and generally 'living the dream' that I really regret making the choices that I did as a young lad.

INSIDE THE ACADEMY GKs

MCR - MCA - DT - NL - OM

With appearances in tournaments such as the prestigious Premier Cup, Matt Campbell is a 16-year-old academy goalkeeper who has recently secured a 2-year contract with Bolton, after spending most of his youth within the world-famous Manchester United academy setup. He is also involved in the Engalnd U15 and U16 sides... We caught up with him to find out more about the trials and tribulations of the 'cut-throat' academy business, and what it's like for goalkeepers within this.

How, and when, did you come about signing for MUFC?

Initially, I was playing for my home team, Wigan school boys, and a Manchester United scout actually came down and watched me a couple of times.

Fortunately, he was sufficiently impressed over a period of time and after a few games he approached me and asked me to come along to a goalkeeper open-day at Carrington with Eric Steele.

From then, I was singled out as a candidate they were interested in, and I began doing extra sessions with the squad. After a rigorous trailing period, I finally signed on the following Easter.

It was obviously quite a major process but that's understandable, looking back, with the sheer numbers involved in the process.

What is the biggest aspect of academy football that sets it out from the rest of the football setup, in your opinion?

For me, personally, it's the professionalism of the players and the coaches. You can tell as soon as you walk in the door that you're there to do business.

As opposed to Sunday League, where everything is more relaxed and loose, there is always a sense of focus and coaches seem to thrive off the development of their players.

How do you deal with the extra pressure that is accumulated playing academy football?

I think that, when you are under pressure, it all boils down to two major components: you can either sink or you can swim. Some people hate it whilst others thrive on it.

For me, I've learned to thrive off the pressure. Although it's hard when you think about all the time, money and energy that has been put into you as a player, you've just got to

THE ANATOMY OF A GOALKEEPER

be able to believe that you are the best first and foremost. Once you've got this, it's just making sure that you are and repaying this back to the club in the results and development you ultimately produce.

How do you deal with seeing other goalkeepers you know well being dropped out of the system?

It's very tough to see other goalkeepers that you have worked with move on. When I train with goalkeepers, whether it be within the England setup or at club level, I develop a working relationship with them so it's tough to see them not get what they want.

However, football is a cut-throat business and so long as you survive the cut, that's all the matters at the end of the day. Of course: it's nice for your mates to get through it with you, but it's about looking after number one because if you don't then nobody will.

When goalkeepers I know are released or don't achieve as they'd hope, I still keep in contact with them, and try to help when I can.

How have you found that the demands of playing change through the years?

The older you get as a footballer, the more the emphasis on tactics becomes greater.

For example, when you are a younger team if you come out of position, or if you don't organise as a goalkeeper from set pieces, it doesn't matter. When you're older, though, a lot of these responsibilities lie with the goalkeeper and if you don't manage them you'll get the blame!

Whilst football is always liable to change at a moment's notice, what can you be doing now so that you're ready to enter the professional picture 2/3 years' down the line if the opportunity is available?

The main way to get better and ensure you are ready for professional football is to make sure you are always progressing, day upon day, week upon week and month upon month.

A lot of goalkeepers struggle with mistakes. At the highest level, although there are less mistakes, they are so much more costly. So recovering from them is hard.

For me the best thing to do is get on with it, make the next save, and then make sure it doesn't happen again; use them as learning points.

I suppose if you get the mistake side of things sorted mentally, then you'll be pretty well prepared for whatever else professional football will throw at you.

WINNING ISN'T EVERYTHING

MCR - MCA - DT - NL - OM

It is the old mantra sprayed around by coaches, speakers and quote machines throughout the country, but often the saying is forgotten in the high-intensity world of football, where manager's jobs depends on bringing home 3 points, not 1, and player's livelihood on their ability to keep the ball out of the goal. However, is there benefit to be had by stepping back, changing our ideologies and letting things pan out a little differently. Dean Thornton speaks about the recent changes to QPR and why he believes they are for the better:

What is the QPR stance with regard to competition in the academy stages?

At QPR, even with the U21s, we don't worry about winning at all: the goal is to get a player into the first team. Within other clubs, though, winning is everything.

I think there needs to be a massive change in the game from winning matches to, instead, developing quality footballers. Being very honest with you: if you had asked me that question three years ago, I would have given you a very different answer. Winning was why I played football.

But then, two years ago, Chris Ramsey came to the club and started to express and implement his philosophies and ideologies on creating talent.

I really struggled at first because with the U18s, for example, we were winning everything from the Category 2 titles to other cups and tournaments and there is a great feeling that winning brings. However, I look back on it and think about who we actually produced and where they are now...

Chris showed me a presentation and some data, on how they'd produced the likes of Ryan Mason and Harry Kane at Tottenham. He sat me down and basically proved the age-old saying that *"winning isn't everything"* to a point where I was totally convinced.

If you look at the way we go about things now at QPR, we're losing games 5-0, 6-0 and 7-0, and outside people are starting to make comment about how poor the setup must be.

The reason for this, though, is the situations we're putting our players in and the constraints they have within the game. By playing the way we like to play in the academies, we're allowing players to develop, such as leaving defenders 1v1 on set pieces and taking the screener away from in front of the back four. This has a plethora of benefits for the goalkeeper, too, where their shot-stopping, ability to claim crosses and distribution is really highlighted.

We might be losing a lot more games than we're winning, but the long-term benefits for the players cannot be overstated.

What is the importance of not focusing on winning and why should grassroots coaches adhere to this?

At a grassroots level, you can understand the coaching scenario when your U11 team are winning 1-0 down at the local park and the manager all of a sudden thinks that it's all about him. He turns into a little José Mourinho, substituting off his weaker players and parking the bus with his strongest team out there.

In reality, we've got to make sure each player gets a certain amount of minutes, for sure. You never know whether these players are going to be late developers or not – the ones sitting on your bench as the weakest may be the ones who have the best chance of playing professionally 10 or 15 years down the line, so to discount them like that isn't necessary or fair at a grassroots level.

How do you work with late developers in this sense at QPR?

We have a relatively similar situation in our academy system now. We've got one lad

who's U15, going into U16 and he's 5"4. For me, he's the best player in our entire academy. At a younger age, though, where winning is everything, he just wouldn't get the ball.

Physically, he still wouldn't now, but we can recreate opportunities and environments in training to accommodate that and, because he's so intelligent and so many steps ahead of the game, he can check shoulders, play early and get the ball in between lines and find pockets of space.

With a winning mentality, it's all about the big lads and their physical prowess. Take that approach, and what would happen to Lionel Messi? Would he have been given the same opportunities if he was English? I don't know. I think this is a huge English problem: we're not technically as good as other nations.

Do you think this will change moving into the future?

I don't think it will. From a grassroots and U18 point of view, we have the league system, where you can see that one team jut battered another 4-0. Also, all it takes now is one click of a button on social media from an ignorant fan that says something like "Look at how Charlton just destroyed Doncaster", and you've got all kinds of insults flying around that become very hard for young players to combat - if a player has Twitter and loses a game, they can be abused by a total random stranger, especially these days with the Category 1 and Category 2 titles.

The only way in which we could change it is by cutting out leagues, just playing 90-minute or 40-minute games. Realistically, I don't think that will ever happen.

Without this emphasis on winning, do we lose out on teaching players how to win games?

We can certainly teach game management skills without necessarily being in a match. At QPR, we do a lot of work around setting scenarios up where teams are 2-0 up, with a few minutes to go, for example, and then we speak about what they need to do to ensure that win and follow it through. And the same vice versa, as well: the other team may be 1-0 down and then we start to see the deliberate differences in the way they play.

We do also teach it through tournaments, which are the only ways at QPR we play competitively and to win with our youth ages. We don't worry about it from about U16s down, but up the years we do compete in tournaments and go out there trying to win. We'll still set individual targets for each player and stick to our normal style of play, but we might start to look at the opposition and think about how we can exploit their potential weaknesses.

COACHING CORNER

The role of the coach has progressed exponentially over the past 30 years as we begin to delve deeper into the science behind developing top-class athletes throughout all of the development pathways. Here, a multitude of world-renowned coaches, lead tutors and other industry experts share their opinion on the workings of the modern goalkeeper coach and how you can help your goalkeepers ultimately develop and succeed in the long-run!

BW — **Bobby White** - Team GB Handball Goalkeeper and Captain at the London 2012 Olympic Games

WB — **Wayne Brown** - Oxford United Goalkeeper Coach

NL+DT — **Nick Levett + Dean Thornton** - As already featured

BF — **Ben Franks** - Student with First Class Honours degree in Sport, Coaching and Physical Education

MP — **Mick Payne** - England C Team Goalkeeping Coach and founder of the famous '*Art of Saving*' camp

TE — **Tony Elliott** - England Futsal Goalkeeper Coach and previous professional goalkeeper

THE ROLE OF A COACH

BW - NL - DT - MP - BF - WB - TE

Whilst this may seem like a painfully straight-forward question, so many 'technical instructors' or 'babysitters' believe that they are coaching without actually doing so. In one of many features from FA Talent ID Manager Nick Levett, we discuss what it means to be a coach and the unrivalled importance of understanding your players:

In your opinion, what is a coach and what does it mean to be coaching?

I wouldn't say that, before the last 5 years or so, I had actually coached. Before then, it was a variety of things from organising football matches to being a technical instructor, but it wasn't until recently that I've really started to understand what coaching actually is.

And that's because it's not about the game. It's about your athletes as people... We just happen to use football as our pathway for making them better as a person.

Too many coaches can't recognise this and the fact you need both parts and that a kid, in one context, is a footballer. In another, when they're at home, for instance, they're just a person, though

They're always a person and we need

to recognise the importance of that as an aspect and understand that football is just our gateway into this improvement.

I think that this is something we're not great at in general coaching at all.

I was in Vancouver a couple of weeks ago and a lot of the coaches got very hung up on the X's and the O's of football and how this player would move to here as the ball moved to there.

Very simply, I said that's all very well in theory. However, if one of the kid's dogs died that morning, they might not want to do it, enjoy it or take anything at all positive out of it!

I remember that I did a session at Fulham in December 2013, all setup to work on counter-attacking. It was going to be brilliant, 90 minutes on it, all planned and ready to go. Then, I remember, at the start of the session, one of the kids said to another that Father Christmas didn't exist.

You can forget the next 90 minutes of counter-attacking because I'm now firefighting how some U9s kid's world has just fallen apart. It's a prime example of how you can forget about the X's and the O's and people need to recognise that it's way beyond just the mechanics of the game – it's the mechanics of people.

It is partly just what the view of the world looks like from a coach's perspective. If you're an U18 coach at a professional club who thinks that you're judged by whether you win the FA Youth Cup or not, you're going to have a very different approach to a grassroots coach at U7s/U8s in a really deprived inner-city area who's just looking at giving these guys a better chance.

It's not for me to tell people how they should view the world by any means, but it's about understanding people. I think a lot of coaches need to realise that.

If we move this forward, then, what are the major things you're looking for in a coach?

When I look for an expert coach, I'm looking at 4 different things:

1) Personality of the coach:
This is often the kind of thing we are never taught. So, for example, when were you ever taught to be more humble or kinder?

You hope your personality pulls you through that, but it's definitely about you as a person and this is so important for your athletes too.

2) Relationships that you build:
This can be with your players and should always be a two-way relationship so that the kids can come and ask you things too...

I know coaches with relationships that are so one-way that people are scared to ask them a question! It's also about relationships with parents, backroom staff and ultimately anyone who may work with the kids.

3) Knowledge of the game:
Obviously the knowledge of whatever it is you're teaching is imperative, because this is the fundamental pin that allows you to develop your athletes and grow them as people, too.

4) Philosophy and coaching culture:
For example, adjusting things such as when we ask questions, how we ask the questions and overall how the session is structured.

If you're solely giving drill and unopposed practice for your kids, you will probably get a very different end product than if you're game-based and ask the kids questions.

One will give you short-term performance and one will help you to develop a footballer. You've just got to choose where you want to be.

PADS, PROS & PERFORMANCE

BW - NL - DT - MP - BF - WB - TE

Since his playing career, representing a multitude of English teams, Wayne Brown has moved into the coaching arena, taking over the reigns of the first team goalkeepers at League One side Oxford United a couple of years ago. He gives us a behind-the-scenes look at life for the goalkeeper and coach at one of England's most forward-thinking, innovative and progressive football clubs:

Officially, what is you role within OUFC?

My job is that I'm head of goalkeeping at Oxford United. This means that I cater for – or oversee – the U8s right through to the U16s and then coach the scholars, youth teamers and first team goalkeepers during the day.

I'll have a set plan of the sort of things that I want to work on through the week with the goalkeepers, depending on the types of games we're playing at the weekend and what we, the backroom staff, feel the goalkeepers need to work on most in preparation for that.

One example, I remember, was that we were playing Wimbledon last season. They had three big guys and kept putting high balls into our goalkeeper, who was getting smashed up and absolutely bombarded.

However, we knew that this kind of game was coming so we'd actually worked on it for the whole week in advance. Everything from simulating the long throw to using pads to give the stimulus of players challenging you in the box made sure everything was very game-realistic and that they were as prepared as possible for the match.

If you were to breakdown the plan of what you were doing on a daily basis, what would it look like?

Throughout the week, the first team goalkeepers won't know exactly what we're doing, but it'll all be setup for the game on Saturday.

On Monday and Tuesday we'll normally have quite an overload on plyometrics and strength work, maybe with a double session thrown in there too. It will be an incredibly intense workout and they're normally blowing by the end of it.

Wednesday the first team won't be in but the scholars will be so we may well do some work with them.

When we move forward to Thursday and beyond, we start to introduce a lot more of the technical bits and pieces, preparing them more directly for the game but also toning down the physical work involved, too. This is also the point that we give them a much better idea of what they can expect from the game on Saturday, whereas before this point (even though we were adjusting our training to suit it) they might not necessarily have known 100% what the situation was calling for.

We have to make sure they're prepared, at the end of the day, because there's nothing worse than going into a game and being absolutely shelled with balls coming into the box and thinking to yourself that you had no idea that the onslaught was going to occur.

What other things do the goalkeepers have and use to make sure they're ready for the game?

They've all got their own little iPads, which they can use to analyse the team they're about to play and watch videos etc... We give them every opportunity to know what's likely to be happening on the Saturday, whether that be sessions with Dan Bond (our performance analyst), work in training or watching videos off their own back.

In all honesty, though, we're not psychic so we can't be 100% sure about how things are going to pan out. Sometimes plans can go totally out the window come 15:00

match day!

What about as a pre-game warmup? What kind of things are you doing there...

The goalkeepers actually get to put together their own pre-match warmup. Each goalkeeper is different from the next and it's totally down to what they feel like they need to work on.

They'll put it on paper and we'll have a chat about it. I might suggest that we should tweak it a little bit to get at least some kind of a sweat on, but at the end of the day it's predominantely up to the goalkeepers.

What's it like working with elite professionals on a daily basis?

It can be hard, sometimes, because you're working on the smallest of details to changing their game. With the young goalkeepers, it's great, because you can remould them however you like, but with these lads it's literally a case of maybe the position of one foot or some other minute detail being slightly off that you'll have to take from the game and then work on further.

Everything we do is filmed and so I suppose there's a much bigger emphasis on my role as a coach to analyse and probe the goalkeepers as opposed to making big technical differences and advancements as we might see in the younger or less professional ranks.

I'm quite fortunate in that the goalkeepers will spend a good hour or so with me every day. We'll usually go out about 45 minutes before everyone else, just to make sure that they're ready for the small-sided games or finishing practice when it comes to it, because every goalkeeper knows that there's nothing worse than being chucked into a drill without any warmup or opportunity to get yourself prepared for the intense action that will follow.

Building on this, what's the environment like on the training pitch?

It's good - very enjoyable. I've been very fortunate not to have had any idiots yet, and I'm happy about that... There's always at least one in the workplace!

My goalkeepers are always quite passionate and I do like them to be opiniated as well, so we can discuss what we're doing and – from my personal angle too – see if there are any areas that we can improve.

People will say it time and time again, but it's so true that coaching is all about having a connection and managing the people first. We'll go out for a bite to eat at lunchtime once a month, just to have a chat, and occasionally I'll take them on the odd night out, too! At the bottom line, we've got to have fun. If you're not having fun and you're not enjoying training, you might as well find another job, in my opinion...

Is your relationship with the goalkeepers better than the other coaches relationship with outfield players, then?

Yes. It has to be. I'm the comfort blanket, really, within the coaching staff. When I was playing, I always found myself looking for my goalkeeper coach in the dressing room because they're the ones who will stand up for you when the manager is giving you bucket loads of abuse. Of course, the goalkeeper coach has to be truthful, but maybe in more of a father figure way than any of the other coaches.

How included are you in talks with the rest of the coaching staff with regard to getting new goalkeepers onboard?

I'm very much included, I think. You'll see just recently we signed Simon Eastwood, who was actually the top goalkeeper from our shortlist so Michael Appleton (OUFC manager) and the others do let us compile a list.

We'll speak to the backroom staff, other goalkeeper coaches and scouts to get a good sort of idea about what these goalkeepers are like and then put that forward to Michael, who can make a decision about what options he'll pursue from there.

Of course, this might not always hold true and occasionally the gaffer may choose to go for someone else but I'll put in a list of what I want and so far we've managed to do alright in getting it!

What about on a day-to-day basis about the performance of the goalkeepers?

We'll probably speak every morning. It might just be a casual meeting walking to the pitches, but sometimes – if there's been a big issue on the Saturday, for example - we might even speak on the phone before we get to the Monday.

You've got to be careful there, though, because 99 times out of 100 people aren't going to be happy if the goalkeeper has made an error on the Saturday and the manager himself may be absolutely livid. Sometimes it is good to wait until the Monday to sit down and have a proper chat, going through things more logically and objectively.

At Oxford, we're very fortunate to have someone like Derek Fazackerly as assistant coach who's very much a *"been there, done it, got the t-shirt"* kind of guy!

He manages to calm everybody down and then we'll start speaking and looking at if there's anything we need to change urgently.

PSYCHOLOGICAL COACHING

BW - NL - DT - MP - BF - WB - TE

Many coaches will cite the psychological side of the game as one of - if not the - most important weapons in a goalkeeper's arsenal. Whether it be to remain composed whilst being bombarded by crosses in the last minutes of the game or having to put up with 45 minutes of constant, unrelenting and full-throttled abuse, it can often be the making or breaking of any young goalkeeper. Here is how it is dealt with in the academy setup, from Dean Thornton once more:

Mentally, are there many issues that the coach has to deal with?

I thoroughly believe that the goalkeeper coach has to be a psychologist, too.

The goalkeepers will ask you all sorts of questions and confide with you about their problems where maybe they wouldn't with the outfield coach because there isn't that same connection. The bond between the goalkeeper and coach is vital and can play a big part in the psychological side of the game.

In all honesty, there are an awful lot of things that I have to deal with on a regular basis...

As goalkeepers, we deal with the strangest experiences, where you could play in front of 30,000 fans, having to stick to a certain area of the pitch and where the fans behind the goal could well be calling you some not very nice things. The outfield players can get away from it a bit more as they move around the pitch, but the goalkeepers are isolated to this one specific area.

Can it be difficult to work on the psychological aspects of the game?

It's hard to work on the psychological side because you can't really measure it. As coaches, we can pull on our own personal experiences as much as possible to try and help the goalkeepers through the dificult periods where we can.

We actually have a number of part-time psychologists involved at QPR now, who can work with all of the players, right through from the first team also down to the foundation phases if they require it, at their parents' discretion.

Can we make goalkeepers too mentally soft, though?

I think that the whole psychological game is massive and our growing understanding on it is helping us to avoid missing out on an abundance of top-class talent.

If a player is struggling in training or whatever, whereas before we might have written it off and just told him to 'man up' or show some more grit, we're now being much more open-minded about the fact that they might have had issues at school or at home and, therefore, that these have to be accommodated for and facilitated in coaching.

On the flip side, though, when a goalkeeper is playing in front of 35,000 people, we need a goalkeeper who is mentally strong enough to deal with the abuse that is being thrown at him and focus on the game in hand. I have some great discussions with the psychologists about whether or not the current setup, for goalkeepers as much as any other position, is creating soft players.

How do we create these environments for goalkeepers?

You can't create these kind of scenarios in academy football, you'd lose your job very quickly if so. It takes a lot of thought from coaches and psychologists to avoid players having too many excuses.

My opinion on the matter has changed, again, in the past year. Looking at the top end (professional development phase),

you've got to put goalkeepers into a stage where they might be fatigued and where things aren't necessarily going right for them.

A lot of the psychologists talk about creating stable environments. Personally, my response to that is that it's great, bringing up a goalkeeper through this stable environment to create a stable player...

Until they have to go and train with the first team and are met by Joey Barton, that is! As you can imagine, he certainly doesn't mince his words and is very open about what he says to the players. If you've just come out of a pristine, stable and secure academy system this may be pretty tough to deal with, even if helpful in the long-run.

But, then again: how do you create that in the academy so that your goalkeepers are prepared? What defines mental toughness? It's the million pound question, for sure.

I think that these moments really are the sink and swim times. You can be the best in the world tactically, technically and physically, but that doesn't mean you're going to be a professional footballer.

Of course, this is my opinion only at the end of the day but something that's definitely a healthy discussion to have.

'RIVERS OF THINKING'

BW - NL - DT - MP - BF - WB - TE

For our final feature in the book with FA Talent ID manager Nick Levett, we totally shake things up, looking at his infamous blog post on coaching goalkeepers, the current drawbacks and the perennial issues that face coaching as a whole.

It sparked a lot of controversy in the goalkeeping world, but the opinions are valid – nonetheless – and offer a pragmatic and candid view on the goalkeeping world from the outside.

What are the issues with goalkeeping that you outlined in your blog?

Firstly, I always thought that our goalkeepers spent way too much time away from everyone else, only calling them back when we had a game or a shooting-style practice and I think that was rubbish!

They'd go off, 200 yards away into 'Compost Corner' and we'd have no idea about the information they were getting, with no links to the games or relationships in the team.

But, also on that, there was no relation to working with players. So, for example, where your starting position is, getting to know the angles better, the state of the game and all things like that as well. Overall, it was just way too much time in isolation and not

preparing them for game-specific situations. It was something that I had a big issue with, certainly.

We had one goalkeeper coach who didn't want to coach the full team, I'd have to absolutely batter him to get him over and do a session, then we had another one who was great and I could throw him in to work with the team and he was brilliant.

The bottom line was that I wanted the goalkeeper coach to work with the team, helping the team to understand the game from the goalkeeper's perspective.

In which case, what were you looking for from your goalkeeper coach?

For me, the goalkeeper coach has to be an integral part of the overall coaching staff, and not just an extra.

Dropkicking balls at kids from 10 yards for 45 minutes will give you a return of some description but whether it's the return you're really after? Who knows?

If you do that, you'll have a goalkeeper who is very good at catching dropkicked balls from that particular distance, but what happens when a defender runs across the line or it comes through somebodies legs.

There are loads of things that you can't plan for and come from the game naturally. I think that you have to put them into the game.

How can we apply and work these ideologies into the game?

The thing is for me is perception and action coupling. Perception is seeing something and then action is the steps I'm going to take to do it.

For example: the ball has ricocheted off the defender and, therefore, I must move in a different way to get to the ball. However, the cues and triggers of that look totally different to an isolated goalkeeper coach.

If you just do the action (i.e a second server) you haven't actually got that trigger, and therefore from a learning perspective it doesn't stack up.

Introducing obstacles/cones/water bottles is still not perfect, because with players in front of you, you don't know whether that player is going to leave the ball, block your view, touch it in the other direction, for example, but it's an awful lot better...

Again, the randomness and unorthodox nature of a game gives you that. I do get that it's not practical and difficult to repeat, I get

all of that, but maybe we need to have a think about how we can change things.

You also made distinct reference in the blog to the use of cones in footwork... Tell us more about your views here.

Again, building on this, I've never seen a cone on a pitch. It's like mannequins, for me. I could play against mannequins in the Premier League because they don't move! It's very easy...

We look at this the wrong way: "the goalkeeper coaches who I look up to in the club do this, and therefore so should I". And that is a perennial problem in coaching full stop.

I think that we have to flip it on its head and look at situations that we've already seen and work back from there. We talk about Déjà vu, but we need 'Vu jàdé'. Take how we've already seen it and flip it in a different way. So, in the same way that somebody like Peter Kay would look at things that happen in a normal, observational way of life and flip that on its head, that's how we need to be looking at coaching.

A goalkeeper running through a ladder and doing 'fast feet', have you ever done that in a game?

If you are moving yourself in a position to get set to deal with a shot, you're going to get there as quickly and as efficiently as you can... You just wouldn't use little steps, in the way they're trained on. So why do it in practice?

If it is shifting yourself backwards, to tip a ball over your head, then maybe for some goalkeepers it might be little small steps, but for others that can just take three big strides, again, this kind of 'footwork' isn't the best solution.

Once more, it all goes back to understanding the individual dynamics of the players you're working with.

That's the other issue with ladders: it changes every person's running gate to be exactly the same. Now, your running gate will be very different to mine, so why try and create somebody's running gate to be exactly the same?

It's all about efficiency and effectivity of movement to solve the problem, which is getting to the 6-yard line in order to narrow the angle for an impending striker. Is it explosive strength that might help to solve the problem instead? Or is it some other kind of skill?

For me, it's not a case of stopping it entirely but instead asking yourself "if the needs of the game don't warrant that behaviour, then why am I doing it?". People maybe don't reflect on their goalkeeping enough, they just go back to "well, we've always done it this way".

What sort of advice would you give to goalkeeper coaches when it comes to session planning?

If you've been in goal, and you've played the game, how did you do it and what did it look like?

You can watch footage of the likes of Buffon, Neuer and Hart and they all will have done it subtly differently.

No shock – they're all individuals!

It's the skills you've got as a coach to meet the individual needs of that particular goalkeeper, most certainly not a one-size-fits-all approach, which will dictate your overall success.

Right, so we're talking here about making sure the drills are always match-specific?

Exactly, this is all in the same way that goalkeeper coaches always give the trigger of 'yes' and drop the ball before they serve it... Why?

I've never seen a centre-forward in a game tell the goalkeeper "yes, I'm about to shoot', so that the goalkeeper thinks "oh alright... I better get set now"... Of course not. They react off the ball, the movement of the ball and the striker's hips, striking foot and non-striking foot, in a real implicit way of learning.

So you have to think about the path of the ball for the goalkeeper when it's being dropkicked in, too.

It's going to be dropped down to his foot, and then move towards the goalkeeper as it's kicked. Well, in a game, how many balls drop like that, and then move forwards?

Rarely. Very rarely.

Often, it will come from a different direction, into the forward (who is stood in a different position) at different heights. You watch the next 10 shots at the next game you watch and I bet every single one of them comes from a different angle, is delivered in a different way, is shot in a different style and arrives at the goal at a different height or part of the goal to the one before.

So why do we think that repetition, repetition, repetition, is going to build a goalkeeper that can deal with the constraints of the game?

What is the answer you get from goalkeeper coaches when you challenge them on this?

I ask the question all the time and it was something that I never really got an answer too... One coach said "well, it's just a case of warming up their hands"...

What a load of nonsense that is, we're just not preparing them for the sport they're about to deal with. One thing that could easily be changed would just be serving the ball from feet, instead.

It's like Rory McIlroy getting to the first tee and doing a couple of half golf swings. He doesn't do that.

He's been to the driving range for an hour before and hit shots that look like the shots that he's going to go and hit for the next four hours of his working life.

The goalkeeper warmups mentioned above are probably more like my warmup for golf, which is a bacon sandwich before I start, swinging the club a few times around my shoulder and thinking that I'm going to go and hit the ball like Tiger! It just doesn't happen like that.

I think that a lot of the problem goes back to coaches and understanding why you do stuff, it's having that self-reflection and awareness of it.

As I mentioned earlier, it's not about totally scrapping these traditional methods, but instead thinking "are they really necessary?" and "is there anything more effective I can be doing with my goalkeepers?".

You can find Nick's blog, filled with his own rambles as well as those from other sports figures at www.riversofthinking.com.

BRIDGING THE GAP

BW · NL · DT · MP · BF · WB · TE

On maybe a rather different tangent to some of our other coaching figures, Ben Franks has just graduated with First Class Honours from Oxford Brookes University. He provides an invaluable scientific insight into the world of goalkeeper coaching, understanding and highlighting the practical theory to produce the best goalkeepers in the long-term.

Tell us a little more about yourself and what your degree is in...

My degree was Sport, Coaching and Physical Education but I suppose my dissertation will give you the best sort of idea of what we're looking at. The technical name of it was 'Affordance Driven: A Portent Beckoning for an Ecological Perspective to Pedagogy in Practice'.

Instead of looking at an isolated attribute of a player, we'd look at the game as a global world, and then try to establish why things happen within that. Essentially, we were reverse engineering the complex system behind the game of football and working back from there.

If you go and observe how nature behaves, organisms react off different stimuli and this is what we were trying to recreate in coaching: a lion instinctively chases down and hunts its prey, so why can't we teach footballers to do the same?

It was more of an angry rant than anything else, but it's been received fairly well and the overall outcome was that we need to stop drilling kids to perform certain tasks and instead let them find and explore themselves.

It's the whole nature vs nurture argument: children learn how to walk without being taught, they just model and receive information and stimulus, naturally picking up triggers, so why can't we model this within coaching?

What is your current view of coaching, as a whole?

Look, to put it simply: I could stand 10 yards away from the goal and volley a ball in, calling "great work", or something similar. This is categorically wrong and, unequivocally, no evidence supports its benefit and yet we still do it.

We coach from myth, ideology and traditional practice and anyone who tries to challenge this gets shot down for being some weird, left wing lunatic [sic!!]. The whole isolation from the ecology of the game is what is really driving down the performance of goalkeepers.

I'm sure we'll all remember the Joe Hart blunder *(actually the day before this interview was recorded!)* and everyone is saying it's because he's too hyped or too inconsistent. It's nothing to do with that.

Instead, it's more likely because he's been coached badly recently, with isolated and unopposed drills, lacking stimulus or game context which means that, when in this game situation, he's struggling to react at the pace of a world-class game.

It's just a case of having goalkeepers responding to cues, triggers and affordances from within their environment as oppose to the coach saying "Joe: I'm going to volley this ball to the top-corner, you're going to save it and then run over to the other corner and make a second save into the hands".

I think I could do that, if I knew where the ball was going, for sure.

Take Buffon, though, these incredible saves through the Euros: he was able to do that because of decades playing time and learning to respond to the stimulus in his environment that meant he could react in that way to make the save.

Of course, it's only my opinion, but it's something that really bugs me and we certainly need to get to the bottom of.

Given this, what are the issues you see now with goalkeepers as a result of this style of coaching?

All Premier League goalkeepers these days look very good in goal; they do the right things and they're technically excellent but they lack the ability to make decisions. This is because they're not allowed to think in training. Or, also, coaches give the goalkeeper the illusion they're making the wrong or right decisions...

The best example I've seen was at a professional club: they were doing a crossing practice where the coach would cross it in and the goalkeeper would come and claim the ball among a couple of players running across him which, in isolation, is an alright drill.

The issue, however, was that the goalkeeper was then told to make a 'quick decision' and throw the ball out to one of two static mannequins either side of the pitch. There's no decision there at all...

It just wastes time and absolutely baffles me!

So you can just do very basic things such as using your feet instead of volleying the ball in. It's all about perception and action coupling. We play against feet in a match, so let's train against feet!

You can still keep your goalkeeper in the goal, with the other two as servers, (and maybe a defender in there to jockey as well) but instantly it's so much more game like when we're keeping that stimulus moving and changing. It also takes the emphasis off the coach serving all the time, which is maybe not the best thing.

A lot of the work I do with goalkeepers is very game-based, or we use lots of rotations in drills to recreate that game situation.

The important thing really is that we afford the key behaviours required for that session and therefore we'll put in place the required constraints for the goalkeeper to suit. It's trying to get the goalkeepers to react around triggers.

It's simple, yet quite complex at the same time. All you need to do is setup what I call a 'Playground of Affordances', where there is so much information and triggers available to goalkeepers that is maybe funnelled through to them but certainly not dictated.

Say, for example, a 4v4 game with a goalkeeper on each side of a square pitch...

If you want goalkeepers to improve at saving shots from a long range then you make the pitch bigger and the shots will naturally come from further out.

If you want the goalkeepers to work on smothering the ball, bring them in closer together and you'll force more 1v1 work when players are through on goal.

Behaviours, then, will be picked up through the environment and goalkeepers develop in the long-term.

Another example, if we were looking at low diving saves, would be that we'd set up an environment with standard goals, a triangle-spaced pitch (with free play in the middle) and then a goalkeeper on each side.

We'd then have, in the corner of each goal, another small goal and the attackers would know that, if they can score in this, they would get five points, compared to one from any other area of the goal.

We're then driving shots towards the corners, thus creating more behaviours of reacting to shots heading towards the corners but also varied in that the players can shoot at any part of the goal, as in a match situation.

We call it 'chaordic' – it's chaos but organised at the same time.

I genuinely think it's easier. We try to overcomplicate things all the time. Instead, we need to be complex.

We think that sessions are great because they look good and there are 12 cones for the goalkeeper to touch before he gets to make the save and he makes lots of movement but it's not necessarily needed because we're creating non-functional movement patterns.

Typical in goalkeeping is the idea of side-stepping around the cone before saving the ball. Coaches will defend it with the old "yeah, but we're working on footwork" where, in reality, if I was going to catch a ball I'd just catch it.

The whole footwork argument is nonsense, too, because footwork requires game-situations for goalkeepers to find their most efficient way of moving towards the ball.

I think that all we need to do is set up a game with a couple of affordances, and it will naturally happen. Yes: coach. Put your coaching points in too, that's all fine.

But we can do that much better if we are watching the session live as oppose to observing a drone catch a ball, if that makes sense.

Working with this, then, is there a correct way for goalkeepers to move or make saves - is this what we need to get away from?

There is certainly no right or wrong way.

There are a huge number of different methods we can use to save the ball, even if they do revolve around the same points. I would save it differently to you because we've got different movement patterns, different anatomies and have had a whole factor of arguments and cultural differences.

Another thing that we really need to get into the heads of grassroots coaches is that we need to understand the limitations and strengths of our individuals.

For example, if the goalkeeper is the smallest player on the pitch, is it really sensible for him to come for a cross? Probably not, but he is still shouted at when he doesn't and the danger averted another way.

You've got to understand that each goalkeeper will manage the game differently for their own capabilities. Look at De Gea, as one example, and the fact that no two players have the same free-kick, too: why can't we accept this is the case with goalkeeping?

Transition slightly... As a coach, how would you integrate goalkeepers into sessions?

I think that we need to reduce the amount of isolated time our goalkeepers are spending as goalkeepers. Instead, play them as outfield players.

I hate, personally, the whole 10 outfield players and one goalkeeper thing. There are 11 players on the pitch, the only difference being one of them can use their hands in a certain area.

They'll learn how to play in goal during your macro-phases or in small-sided games, but for general squad work, just put them out on

pitch.

The game is changing and evolving, with goalkeepers touching the ball three times with their feet for every one with their hand. That's a big ratio.

We still regard goalkeepers such as Manuel Neuer as eccentric, whereas really his style should be the norm in this ever-improving game.

So, what would you do now to try and improve the situation?

Without trying to be the overlord of it all, I think there needs to be a much smaller gap between actual, practising coaches and the ivory tower academics.

People like Nick Levett need to be the bridge between taking the theory that we know to be most effective and then replicating that within coach education programmes for coaches. I think that's something that's not going on at the minute.

There are so many academic studies and journals, not only within sports and football but also looking a bit beyond that.

Universities like Oxford Brookes are doing lots of great work in this area, helping to practically support, as well as further, the theory that we've got coming in. Additionally, we're starting to get there with games in coaching. The England DNA, despite its recent shortcomings, is starting to encompass more of a games-based approach for the younger age groups, but there's also been a big push on the psychological side of things too.

There are studies coming in about working with affordances and that side of things from learning theorists as well, looking at complex systems and how objects or people will interact with one another.

It's all about how teams can maybe begin to become more of a unit than a variety of isolated positions.

For goalkeeping, there isn't really much

specific, though, despite a bit of information stimulus, but that's all around penalties and static situations.

Having said that, it is quite good in the sense that it explores how goalkeepers are looking at things like body shape, back-lift and other language from the kick takers so there's definitely aspects we can take from all of these studies.

Is the answer, therefore, to have more information out there for coaches?

I think yes and no at the same time.

Yes, in the sense that we could do with more papers supplied, maybe starting to look at different areas of the position but no, in the idea that we can (and need to!) also spend a lot of time cross-theorising between studies.

For example, one of the undergraduate papers that I did took a lot of theories from Maths and Physics to show that you can predict everything that would happen in a game using some sort of binary code.

It was kind of a bit weird, but it also made perfect sense. We can predict every action that a player could possibly make, as long as we can decipher the relevant variables (where he likes to move, the opposition around him etc.)...

It's just a shame that there's something stupid like five billion variables a second to work from!

However, if we can get this down to a few thousand desired behaviours (by closing down certain behaviours and changing the environment) then we can actually predict every action within a game of football.

I mean, obviously, the paper wasn't particularly applied, but it does kind of make sense that we can really implicitly stagger sessions and understand what's going on, without it seeing as such from the outside.

Encompassing all of this, where do you see the world of coaching going forward?

Coaching as a whole is moving towards the right direction.

The England DNA is a good step. In terms of academic work being used, there is very little chance of it coming across at the minute as academics are still writing for themselves and coaches still think that they're pompous idiots.

In terms of goalkeeper coaching, that's never going to change if we keep going by the same mantra of *"You played in goal and therefore you can coach goalkeepers"*...

I've seen some brilliant ex-professional goalkeepers, but then, unfortunately, there are also some bad ones too.

I think the problem is that too many people think that they played in goal and, therefore, they can automatically coach it too; the coach education system needs to change.

Ex-goalkeepers have the incredible context knowledge that you only get after decades of playing, but they just don't know how to deliver it. At the moment, the courses are very heavily based around context, whereas the goalkeepers may benefit more from actually learning, instead, how to deliver a session.

I think that it needs to be a big shift in focus towards the learning process as oppose to what we're actually coaching – how we can get the points across to the learner without shoving it down their throat.

Tieing it all together, where can coaches find out more about modern approaches to coaching that they can apply to their goalkeeper sessions?

Well, for a start there's my blog! Tim Dittmer, who is the FA Lead National Goalkeeper Coach has got some really good points, and guys like Nick Levett too.

The problem with journals and research is that there is so much technical language out there that it's almost impossibly inaccessible for anyone who hasn't got a degree in it.

You can find a (rather long!) link to Ben's blog and an abundance of insight and perspective on latest sporting events through his Twitter: @ben_4L.

COACH'S SELF-ANALYSIS

BW - NL - DT - MP - BF - WB - TE

Often, it can be incredibly useful for coaches to look back on a training session or the progress of their team/goalkeepers over time, but this can be difficult if you're not sure what to look for. We speak to London 2012 Olympian Bobby White to hear his thoughts on coaches and analysing their behaviour, too:

What is your main belief when it comes to coaching and developing goalkeepers?

My personal belief is that the coach should try to recreate game scenarios in practice as much as possible. Decision making is a vital asset for the goalkeeper so learning to make decisions about narrowing angles, making the right pass or coming for crosses needs to happen in training so that they can draw on those experiences in competitive situations and ultimately develop further for it.

At a grassroots level, how can coaches be developing this philosophy with their goalkeepers, within specific drills and the training as a whole?

Understanding the needs, wants and requirements of any participant should be the number one priority for any coach. Most kids want to 'play' games or participate

in exercises that are fun, demanding and relevant to what they're supposed to be learning.

Some coaches might prioritise the technical aspect of catching; it is not uncommon to see young goalkeepers side-stepping through cones to face a half volley from a coach striking the ball from 5 yards away but does this ever happen in a game?

In terms of supporting motivation for learning, you have to think about 3 key factors in my opinion:

1) Does the participant have ownership or autonomy over what they are trying to achieve, or is the coach telling what to do and when to do it? Can we allow the kids to learn from their mistakes?

2) Can the participant demonstrate competence in the learning outcome? They have to achieve a level of success if they are going to feel confident and continue with the task.

3) Does the participant feel connected to the coach, their team mates and the session? They have to feel that they are welcome and have good relationships – ultimately that will make sure they come back next week!

93

Along similar lines, how important is the reaction of the coach and those around the goalkeepe?

When we are learning new skills like coming to catch a cross, the young goalkeeper will be thinking something along the lines of the 'come or stay?' and the 'catch or parry?' debate, and potentially a couple of other factors too.

Those questions may take a spilt second to be answered but it could be the difference between a successful outcome for the goalkeeper or a negative one (a goal scored for the opposition). You can guarantee that a goalkeeper will make a mistake at some point and this is all a fundamental part of the learning process.

How the coach, players and parents react to this could have a massive impact on the goalkeeper's mentality and approach to dealing the next situation when he/she is called into action: they may begin to shy away for coming for anything or do the complete opposite and come flying out for a ball on the edge of the area.

Either way, we're not encouraging autonomous decisions and ownership of their mistakes so their ability to make these key decisions in high-pressure situations later in their development is likely to be poorer.

The time frame in which those questions are answered will reduce over time and become unconscious rather than conscious but you cannot skip this phase.

As a coach, I have learnt that my body language and feedback at these moments are crucial. We should expect and accept these mistakes will happen and try to deal with them as constructively as possible. A young goalkeeper knows the outcome of a mistake because it usually ends up in his/her goal and they will definitely feel bad about that so we certainly shouldn't exacerbate the situation!

How can coaches look back to analyse and assess their session from the perspective of enjoyment and positivity?

The importance of a fun, positive and appropriate learning environment should not be overstated. Fun can sometimes mean engaging (the opposite to that which is 'boring'!) and it is important to have some expectations around what you will imagine to happen in your session:

Is their laugher? Excitement? Action? Chaos? Confusion? Or is there silence? Static Players? Poor Behaviour?

If we can recognise this, we can start to appreciate what the participants might be experiencing or feeling.

Sometimes, it is worth having a session or two recorded to analyse what we are doing as coaches: How much time are we talking compared to the participants being active? What things are we saying? Are our messages understood? Was my positioning the best it could have been?

Ultimately, it really depends on the coach, the group and what the objectives are but most of the time we would be looking at a few key indicators to see if the environment we have created is fun, positive and conducive to learning:

What is the attendance like? Are the kids coming back week after week?

Do the kids express themselves? Do they talk to the coach and ask questions.

Are they demonstrating improvements? If they are not showing signs of improvement we need to question why and the first question I ask is usually "is it something I am doing?"

What is the general behaviour like in the group: if there is a lot of messing around, this could be because they are bored, not because they lack attention!

Do you have a set guide or approach at all to delivering training drills and ensuring they are appropriate for your athletes?

It's important when developing a practice to consider a plethora of different factors, but the key message is they must revolve around your 'WHO, WHAT, and HOW':

1) First I must consider why this skill or technique is used in a game? E.g. GK 1v1 with attacker, GK has to go hands first to take the ball.

2) I then try to think of a 'game' we can play that will bring those situations out. Hungry Hippos for example is a game we use similar which is similar in style to the

playground classic 'bull dog' but the goalkeepers have to intercept the ball or tackle the players dribbling by going down at their feet.

3) I then have set expectations within the drill in that if I don't see goalkeepers performing this skill regularly, something may need to change and I use the STEP principle as a guide here...

The step principles are a well-renowned metric for adapting tasks to ensure maximum effectivity:

SPACE - IS THE SPACE TOO BIG/SMALL?

TASK - IS THIS TASK RELEVANT TO THE TECHNIQUES WE'RE LOOKING TO IMPROVE?

EQUIPMENT - COULD WE USE DIFFERENT EQUIPMENT?

PEOPLE - IS THIS EXERCISE RELEVANT TO THE AGE AND STAGE OF PEOPLE I'M WORKING WITH?

You can find more about Bobby's work at his Twitter on: @bobby_white_12

YOUR LEARNING ENVIRONMENT

BW - NL - DT - MP - BF - WB - TE

As a coach, especially in the modern era, we have a much greater understading and emphasis upon the importance of creating a positive and conducive learning environment for our sessions in order to get the most out of our athletes. Nick Levett, Mick Payne and Tony Elliott share their views, opinions and top tips on creating this positive learning environment:

NICK LEVETT

When you're coaching, how do you initially try to create a conducive learning environment?

I think it starts even before a ball is kicked - that walk from the car park to the pitches is one of the biggest parts for me. Often, I would time it so I arrive there with some of the kids and this 100m walk – there and then – is where the environment starts.

It might be a conversation with the parent about what's happening at home, what other sports they've been doing etc., or the conversation with the kid as I walk down there.

It could be anything from "oi, it's his bag,

let him carry it", aimed at the parent, to "tell me something exciting that happened today".

I absolutely always have that early engagement with them because as soon as I've done that I can find out where the kids are at: have they had a good day at school or have they been told off by Mum because their room is a mess?

I can't start talking about principles and technical points if the kids aren't in the mood.

We had one kid, I remember, who travelled quite a long way. He'd be sat in the back of Mum's car for a long trip. Some days I'd know that he'd cry all of the way there and not want to be at the session. Not because of the football, necessarily, but because of the journey – he was a very talented kid. I had to know exactly where he was at that day.

We had another kid who would travel from North London, underground, then overground and then a 10 minute walk to the Fulham training ground, on his own, from the age of 9. It was probably the fact that he did it on his own through London, and not many kids would do that, that meant we had to be particular aware of the situation.

The coach I was coaching with at the time sort of went "oh, you're late again", as he turned up 10 minutes over time to a session.

My initial reaction was "woah, you've got no idea what he's been through to get here".

He's got home from school, had to walk to the shop, buy the food, take it home, feed his little sister and then get the train all across London totally alone.

So, definitely, that setting the environment is understanding the kids. If you can't do that, you're not a coach. And then you can start worrying about the football bit.

In session, how do you then develop this positive environment?

There are a number of things we look at when we're talking about coaching such as being player-centred, enjoyable and in a safe environment.

I'm always cautious to use the word fun, when we're talking about elite academies especially: it shouldn't always be fun. It should be enjoyable so that they want to keep back coming but, if you're doing deliberate practice, by definition that isn't fun.

It's stimulating, it hurts your head, it gets you thinking to the edge of your comfort zone – it's not fun. It should have some enjoyable elements, but not just the unstructured

nature of 'fun', even more so when we work up the ages.

At grassroots, though? Absolutely. Fun has to be at the heart of it. And it will be different in different scenarios, of course.

MICK PAYNE

How important is understanding the athletes you're working with and adjusting your tone and delivery to suit this?

I think it's certainly a massive point. I class myself as a coach because I can coach goalkeepers of all levels and abilities, following the mantra of learn, improve and principally enjoy.

For example, when we have our yearly 'The Art of Saving' goalkeeper courses, we have guys from U8 to people in their 40s.

Obviously, the older guys are playing as much for fun and pride but also still – of course – they're trying to get better and then we've got the younger guys who clearly aren't going to have the power or strength to perform to the same level as some of the others.

I say to all of them that the sessions are the same for all of them, but it's the way in which that session is setup which allows me to differentiate between athletes.

Of course, if you've got international goalkeepers, like we work with sometimes, their expectations are going to be much higher.

What is the importance of a positive environment for your players?

There should always be a positive vibe within your training sessions. I don't think you'll find any goalkeeper who'll go out there to try and make a mistake – it's a ludicrous suggestion.

However, we have to look at why we do make mistakes and then look back and analyse this again.

Self-analysis will always be absolutely vital. Allowing your goalkeepers to do something like "*Take three things I did well from that session...*" allows them to remain positive but also reinforces your key coaching points and ultimately helps them take ownership of their learning. I'm also an absolutely massive believer in keeping things positive for your goalkeepers.

For example, we'll always finish on a positive moment, "*One to get you out*" is how we refer to it. It's these quite small and subtle decisions from a coach that means the player goes away feeling that they've finished the session well, as opposed to being down about how everything didn't reach their expectations.

Overall, a philosophy of confidence, making sure you speak to your goalkeepers correctly and really drilling home that positive atmosphere within training and match situations is what you need to be doing in order to instil those vibes for everyone within your long-term player development.

How are goalkeepers encouraged to take ownership?

We encourage goalkeepers to take a journal or a diary to sessions and fill these in with the different sections of goalkeeping and mark their performance after training and matches.

Then, you can have a look and assess, seeing if there are any patterns and these are the bits you can work principally on at training. Building this, it's very much my belief that goalkeepers should maximise their strengths but minimise their weaknesses.

It's vital that the coaches allow and probe the athletes to come to their own conclusions within training sessions, as all types of different learners require different coaching styles to accompany that.

There are times where it has to be coach-led, but at others it's important that, once goalkeepers have experience, they can speak out about what they want to improve on with training as this can be very beneficial to a player's development. As long as it's in the remit of what should be happening then there's no problem – in my opinion – with this being the case.

How do you deal with unrealistic expectations from a manager that may hamper this environment?

I'm at the stage now where I'll question managers, without any problem at all. I think that they'll respect me for that.

We'll have managers who will want their goalkeepers breathing out of their backside and absolutely knackered, thinking they've worked on goalkeeping. Well, no: you've worked on fitness.

But technical form will have really dropped away, you've got to be wary about making fitness over form decisions, especially during the season.

When the exercise a manger has a goalkeeper working on sacrifices all important form for fitness, that's when you have to start questioning their choices.

TONY ELLIOT

What is the most important element of creating a positive environment?

For me, I think that first contact is always vital. W
I.

It might be a well-known quote, but I certainly think it's a massive part of working with people. I'm not saying you have to be all fun and laughter with them all the time, but if you can make people feel comfortable then you're really on your way to making them want to learn and develop, as much as anything else.

Really, it just comes down to always treating people how you would like to be treated or, if I'm working with a young goalkeeper, understanding that I've got 4 kids of my own and trying to treat the youngsters how I would like someone else to treat my kids.

That's the mind-set that I try and go with, but it is important to pitch it as well, depending on who you're working with.

If it's international athletes, there will be times when you have to get down to the nuts and bolts of it and your goalkeepers will need to know that there needs to be an action and that this action will need to have an outcome.

On the other hand, if it's at grassroots level, then maybe we're looking for something slightly different.

Building on that, I think one of the primary roles for a coach, actually, is knowing the people that you are working with. The syllabus might be great, the content might be brilliant but, if you don't connect with the athletes you're working with, it's never going to work.

Therefore, that first connection, contact and session with them is massively important. There are so many things you have to consider; it's not always about the session or the drill, but it is always about the person on the other side of it.

We all come from different backgrounds, have different needs and separate things required to tick our boxes. And that's what a coach has got to understand: it's all about the other person.

As a coach, I know what I've done as a player and the career I had, but I don't need to live off past glories or things that I've achieved. My role now is singularly to help develop, push on and educate the goalkeepers that I'm in contact with, whether that be at an international level, grassroots or the elite academy setup.

My job is to give them a wonderful experience and also to share my knowledge with them. I think that the art of coaching is recognising the what, where, who and when...

There is so much that we have to consider now, as well as a massive amount of responsibility on the coaches.

How has the role of the coach changed over the last few decades to facilitate this conducive learning environment?

I think that coaching has changed massively. The way we deliver sessions, how we share knowledge and generally our demeanour in expressing ourselves is all changing.

Whether that's for the good or not, that's yet to be seen, but I personally have had to adapt to these new changes in the way we educate young people and I would like to think that I have adjusted to that quite well.

Sometimes it's a case of understanding that, if I give people all the information at once, it's going to be too much, and they won't absorb as much of it as they can, so I like to try and drip-feed people information.

If they need it they can have it, if they want it they can have it, but if they don't need it it's the coach's job to recognise this and just hold on to it for that little bit of extra time until they're ready. In the old days, it was very much coach-led: *"this is how it is, so go and do it"*.

If you look at the modern game, though, there are many different ways that we can get the outcome we desire from a unit, group or individual whereas in the past there would be a warmup (probably running laps round the field), followed by a small-sided game, a little bit of work on phases of play, maybe, and that would just be it.

Now, there's much more depth and detail that goes into planning sessions, with a lot more emphasis on players taking ownership of their experience and also using methods that we know to work within the training sessions.

We've also got the fact that coaches understand their roles and responsibilities much better and this means that the collaboration within the team can be far superior to before as they search to solve problems and develop footballers.

Back in the day, goalkeeper coaches would work solely with the goalkeeper. Fast forward to present, though, and the introduction of things such as the England DNA, as well as the natural progression of the game, means that goalkeeper coaches are often expected to influence the whole game, working with the different units to collaborate with the goalkeeper and making sure they understand the relevance and importance of the goalkeeper's influence.

What about the player: how has their role changed in this environment?

As well as that, now, is that the player is encouraged to take a lot of ownership and there is sharing of knowledge, experience and responsibility between both the coach-athlete relationship and also across the backroom staff.

Ultimately, whereas back then it was the coach that was responsible, everyone within your unit is responsible now and this is probably for the better – you're not just relying on one person. I think that the modern way is the way to create something special, certainly.

It doesn't mean that all situations are going to be successful, of course not, but it means that we can share that responsibility as oppose to just burning it on one individual. I'm a big believer, also, that success is a team thing: it's not just about one person, it's about the whole team and infrastructure behind that.

IN-GAME GOALKEEPING

Goalkeeping is a specialised position, requiring specialised actions and decisions. There are an abundance of different techniques, skills and methods that goalkeepers can use from all across the world in order to enhance their game and find out exactly what 'works' for them. We uncover just a small number of these as well as looking at the mental and tactical side of the goalkeeper, too.

EK   **Eric Klenofsky** - Division One American College and NY Red Bulls U23 Goalkeeper

DT   **Dean Thornton** - QPR Lead Academy Goalkeeping Coach and former England Futsal International

NL   **Richard O'Donnell** - Bristol City FC Goalkeeper and formerly of Walsall and Sheffield Wednesday

MB   **Melissa Barbieri** - Former Australia Women's Goalkeeper and Captain and continental cup winner

MP   **Richard Lee** - Former BPL Goalkeeper and owner of GKIcon franchise as well as renowned penalty saver

THE FAMOUS 3:1 GOALKEEPER...

EK · MB · DT · RL · ROD

In the modern game, the requirements of the goalkeeper are changing hugely as we adapt to new styles of play and tactical adjustments. We speak with QPR Lead Academy Goalkeeper Coach Dean Thornton on his opinions on what this means for players and coaches alike:

What does the 3:1 ratio mean for a goalkeeper?

We've already established that goalkeepers play with their feet more, at a ratio of about three events where they're using their feet, compared to every single touch with their hands.

The important thing to do here, though, is to flip it over and look at the goalkeeper coaches. At the minute, they're not recognising this and still not allowing goalkeepers to build up their core skills a lot of the time. Something that I've certainly made an active effort to do with the academy lads over the past year is to make sure that they spend more time with their team.

We'll achieve this by them warming up all together, and then maybe doing some passing work too, before they then come over to myself or one of the other part-time coaches for their dedicated goalkeeper training in every session.

What evidence is there that goalkeepers develop best in this way?

If you look at the England setup of goalkeepers as a whole, and take a look at where the goalkeepers have come from, I think it gives a very telling story.

Look at Joe Hart, who started off at Shrewsbury, Ben Foster, coming from Wrexham, John Ruddy at Cambridge. All of these top English goalkeepers have come through academies where they may well not have had the required facilities or resources required for dedicated goalkeeper coaching at every session, meaning that the goalkeepers will become more adept to playing with their feet and maybe this is what has pushed them above the others.

Again, look at the top teams like Arsenal, Chelsea and Manchester United. How many goalkeepers have actually come all the way through their system to start for the first team? Not many. Maybe before we didn't understand the importance of goalkeepers using their feet, we're seeing these goalkeepers being neglected and left out because they're isolated in their training.

It hits the social corner, too, when they're not training with their team as much and maybe this is another reason some of the big academies boys haven't fulfilled their promise.

Does this mean we'll see a benefit in later specialising goalkeepers?

Yes. The likes of Edwin Van Der Sar, Manuel Neuer and Hugo Lloris didn't totally specialise playing in goal until a much later date than many English goalkeepers.

Academies in England essentially pigeon-hole young goalkeepers, in one sense. Because of the rigours and demands of the academy timetable, these goalkeepers can't go out and play any other sports and, for goalkeepers especially with the hand-eye coordination aspect, playing any sports like volleyball, tennis and basketball can be vital to their long-term development.

For me, it's probably a case of deciding when you're at the age of about 14, and deciding whether you want to be a cricketer, goalkeeper or whatever else it may be.

Why do we specialise English goalkeepers so early on?

It's an interesting one, but I think that maybe the Elite Player Performance Plan (EPPP) has to take some of the blame. They're saying that players have to do a certain amount of football a week in order for the clubs to satisfy the criteria and it really does take away the social life of the player and their ability to play other sports too. But that's the way the FA and EPPP decided to run with it.

Can academies themselves be offering multi-sports for their players?

I don't think that it's productive for the academies to offer multi-sport, but it does need to change. We're saying to kids in the foundation phase that might be exceptional cricketers or rugby players that they have to specialise and stick with football. My problem is that the game is more of a business.

How does this business aspect materialise?

We can offer a 10-year-old at QPR the opportunity to come and play for us, which might be a bit more convenient and more balanced for the player, but then Chelsea may turn around and say they can do the same thing, but with some of the best facilities in the world and paying your parents on a monthly basis, too, but without the multi-sport. What option are the parent and kid going to choose?

DECISIONS IN DISTRIBUTION

EK - MB - DT - RL - ROD

Especially in the modern game, the role of the goalkeeper is pivotal both in attack and defense. Their ability to obtain and release the ball quickly and effectively is by no means an easy feat, but can most certainly put your team on the front foot into the counter-attacking phase, as Eric Klenofsky explains:

How important is decision making for a goalkeeper?

Decision making in any facet of football is massive: if you can think quickly enough and make the correct decisions under pressure, odds are you'll be at least a decent footballer.

Coaches often talk about bringing the ball out of pressure when you're in tight spaces, finding the gaps and creating space for yourself to play. This doesn't change for goalkeepers, all of this remains the same; it's just the context that changes.

What sort of areas of the pitch should the goalkeeper be looking to distribute the ball?

I can remember watching an interview of Tim Howard where he talks about the fact that whichever direction the ball comes from influences your decision as to where you look

first to distribute.

He goes on to explain how the first option should be the opposite side of the field to which the ball came from. So, if you took a cross from your left side, your first question is "can I start a counter attack going up the right side?"

This goes back to bringing the ball out of pressure and creating space: if you take a cross from the left side, odds are that the potential target, or targets, for that cross were coming from the right side meaning defensively the opposition has lost its shape in that moment and there is space for the ball to be distributed towards the right side.

In terms of placement, I would keep the ball out of the middle of the field whenever possible. Like I've mentioned before, you want the ball out of the way of any pressure.

You put your most technical players in the middle of the field because they have the best chance of playing out of that pressure. Getting the ball to the wide guys is the goalkeeper's job going forward. It is more beneficial in terms of attacking and it is more beneficial in terms of defending.

Losing the ball trying to pick out a right winger and losing the ball trying to pick out your defensive midfielder are two completely different scenarios with very different potential outcomes.

If you lose the ball distributing to your centre-midfielder, you could be facing an attempt on goal very quickly. It is much easier to defend and recover for a ball that is lost out wide than it is for a ball that is centrally located for obvious reasons.

What are the different types of distribution and when should the goalkeeper be looking to use them?

If it's close range and the path is clear, obviously a roll should suffice. If it's outside your range for a roll but not far enough to be side volleyed, a throw should be the sort of thing you're looking at.

Anything outside of your throwing range (especially whilst attempting to move quickly for a counter attack) should be side volleyed as accurately as possible. The side volley is your quickest, most direct and most accurate fast-paced distribution choice, although it can take a bit of practice to work accurately.

What are the other things the goalkeeper needs to consider?

In terms of decision making from there on in,

the game will be the decider. What the score is, how your team is playing, how the other team is playing, and the stage you are at in the game are all factors which will help you to construct your decision.

If you're up a goal in the 85th minute and being pressed heavily, slowing the game down and letting your team catch their breath is probably the best option.

On the other hand, if you're 1-0 down and you pick a cross in the 85th minute with two players breaking towards the halfway line, by all means get to the top of the box as quick as you can and distribute the ball as fast as possible.

How can goalkeepers improve their decision making?

Whilst it's easy out of context to put together a 'how-to guide', almost, decision making within distribution is not easy at all.

The best way to improve your decision making is to be a student of the game and absorb as much knowledge about distribution as possible. That means watching the professionals that distribute well and trying to take what they do into your own game.

If it's a case of working similar scenarios into your training drills then so be it, but always ensure that you are thinking actively about the decisions you're making and whether they are necessarily the best route for you.

In terms of improving your distribution, I would say spending more time with the ball at your feet is your best option, getting more comfortable hitting balls to different distances and angles and dealing with different scenarios you might see in a game that should be taken advantage of.

THE SPIN TECHNIQUE

EK - MB - DT - RL - ROD

A favourite of goalkeepers such as Tottenham and France's Hugo Lloris, the spin recovery allows goalkeepers an efficient, effective and impressive way to keep rebounds out of the net. Whilst a very difficult skill to master, its results can pay dividends in moving to the ball quicker and, ultimately, keeping a clean sheet for your side. We speak, once more, to one of the top-ranked U23 American goalkeepers, Eric Klenofsky, on execution of the technique and his favourite technicians:

Tell us a little more about the spin technique and your introduction to it...

The spin recovery technique is one of the most enjoyable techniques to teach and learn.

It is important to note that the spin is used situationally; it is not a one-size-fits-all technique. It will suit some goalkeepers and some situations better than others, so as a goalkeeper we have to make the active decision as to whether or not we will employ it at any given moment.

If I knew where its origination was I would tell you but, to be honest, I haven't got a clue! I assume somewhere within Spanish or South American football.

I see the most goalkeepers from those areas using it and mastering it to the point that they can use it really effectively on match day.

Although I do think it was developed from a South American or Spanish footballing country, some of the best technicians of it in the current day are Hugo Lloris of Tottenham and France as well as Jonathon Bond of Reading and England.

In which situations might goalkeepers look to use the spin technique?

You use the spin as a way to maximise your energy during a change of direction and they seem to be able to do this with real conviction.

For example, diving to your right to make a save and then having to recover back to your left due to a deflection from the rebound, a deflection off a defender or any other scenario you could think of that would cause you to change direction.

Using it effectively, training it and engaging it will all go into the same kind of explanation. So, as I said before, it is all about maximising the energy you've gained through your initial dive and recycling that energy into the change of direction.

That being said, pushing as hard as possible and diving through the first ball is the first step to being able to spin effectively. Once you've dived through the first ball, the immediate priority is to harness that energy and recycle it. You can do this by spinning your legs around using your hips and then back to the spinning point.

I tell my goalkeepers to kick both legs simultaneously towards the direction in which you've just dived whilst, at the same time, twisting your chest in the opposite direction. The harder you kick your legs while just learning this technique, the easier it will be to push your momentum in the direction you want to go in.

How should goalkeepers go about training this?

You train this just like the initial acquisition of anything else: through repetition. Muscle memory is the name of the game for this and you want to practice exactly what I've just described over and over until kicking your legs is no longer necessary and your body's natural reactions take over when the situation calls for it.

The second stage is then its implementation in game-based drills and scenarios, so the goalkeeper can learn the correct situations and scenarios in which they're going to execute the required skill.

It is important to note that this is not an easy technique to master and it is only used in specific situations; trying to force the spin for a situation that doesn't warrant it will only hurt your chances of making the second save.

DEALING WITH CORNERS

BW - NL - ROD - MP - RL - SD

Especially through the later youth age groups and into senior football, the emphasis of managing defensive corners moves towards the list of goalkeeping responsibilities. For his final feature, we speak to Eric Klenofsky on his experience and advice for organising your defensive setup and your positioning, too:

What are the main aspects and decisions to be made within the defensive corner?

Defensive corners are not as black and white as people might tend to think.

To start with, there needs to be a decision made within the team between the goalkeeper, the backline and the coaching staff about how to deal with corners and set pieces in general. The decision of whether to mark man for man or zonally is an important decision that needs to be decided in training.

If you have chosen to go zonally, the position of the zonal defenders is at the team's discretion but everyone within the squad should be made aware of this, regardless of position.

On the other side of the equation, if you have chosen to go man for man, goalkeepers must organise their defence by size and ability. Your best header of the ball that is not one of your biggest defenders should be at the front of the attackers, in my opinion, to guard against the near post run but still with the ability to clear the ball away with his head, too. From there, you should have one of the smaller players on your front post with a man on the back post if you feel that is necessary and have the numbers.

If the opposition sends two to the corner and tries to play short, the first person stepping should be the man covering the front six, the defender covering your front post would then slide into kind of a dual role of covering the front six and manning the front post.

I tell my defenders who are in this role to go an arm's length away from the front post in order to split the different roles beneficially.

What about coming to claim the cross?

Obviously every goalkeeper's range on crosses is a bit different but that doesn't really change how to deal with them. To begin with, your first step should never be forward, that should not be your initial reaction unless you are absolutely positive you are running forward onto the ball. If you take a step too aggressively the ball could be over you and at the back post in a split second.

The question you should be asking yourself no matter who you are is "Can I get to this ball before it drops?"

If the answer is yes, by all means go on and get it. If the answer is no, that should be communicated to your defensive team and you should drop into your set position a bit deeper than your starting point would be for the cross.

Often, you see professional goalkeepers drop all the way to their line trying to buy time to react off the header. In terms of body shape while taking the cross, for anything going towards the back post, your back leg should come up and anything going forward or near post your front leg should come up to help you gain momentum towards the ball fluidly whilst protecting yourself at the same time.

For example, if the corner is from your left side and is hit to the back post, you should crossover step to the ball with your right knee coming up as you go towards the ball.

Each goalkeeper, though, may find something else that works for them so that's an important thing to consider during practice.

Are there any goalkeepers who do this particularly well?

Stoke City and England goalkeeper Jack Butland does this seamlessly. If you are looking for a goalkeeper to emulate, he's your guy. We pick up the back leg in that scenario for two reasons.

First, we don't want to fight our momentum. Picking up your right (back) leg in the scenario just explained will lift you up to the ball much like a high jumper would do to get over the wire they are trying to jump over.

The second reason is to protect yourself. If the service is coming from your left side, that means the opposition trying to attack the corner would be coming from your right side towards the ball and therefore you need your leg best positioned as a barrier between the two of you.

There're many aspects of taking crosses and many different ideas about this is best executed, but this is the basic framework of how to deal with crosses properly that any goalkeeper can take forward and adjust as they choose.

THE SWEEPER KEEPER

EK - MB - DT - RL - ROD

The sweeper-keeper role is one that has developed considerably over the past couple of decades and even more exponentially in very recent years. We spoke to one of the most highly-regarded Football League goalkeepers who chooses to adapt this more aggresive starting position in Richard O'Donnell:

How important is the role of the sweeper-goalkeeper in the modern game?

I think it's a very important role: for your defenders to know that their goalkeeper is right behind them on the front foot, it makes their jobs considerably easier. Some teams like to play a high line which makes it even more important that the goalkeeper is aggressive and bold in their starting position.

I'd like to think that I've always been aggressive and bold in my positioning and I find that, because of it, my decision-making is that little bit more straight-forward. Balls over the top and in behind the defenders are easier to deal with because your decision is almost made up when you're positive in that you'll come for the ball.

What are the key points for the execution of clearing the ball/reacting to a situation?

As I said earlier, being bold and positive makes things easier in my opinion. The balls that you aren't sure about with a deep position become balls that you will naturally come for when higher up. Once you've made the decision to come there are two key things to think about when clearing the ball with whatever part of your body it may be: height and width.

Height always gives you and your defenders time to react regardless of how far it goes. Don't get me wrong, the further the better, but if you get height it gives you chance to get into a good recovery position.

Width is a big one as well... It's obviously harder to score from out wide than it is from the middle of the goal! Getting the clearance high and wide is the safest way to play it.

What sort of guidance do you use to choose your starting position?

I don't tend to have specific areas that I work to, this can change depending on what sort of team you're playing and how they set-up.

Naturally, your defenders will drop off a little more if they're up against a very quick

striker, so it's definitely something that needs thought about for every game you play. It's not only the players you play against that can change your position, though, as the weather can also play a massive part in where you start.

For example, if it's raining or has been raining and the pitch is wet, the ball will obviously come through to you a lot quicker than it would if it's a dry pitch and again, in my opinion, it's an easier decision to make in wetter conditions as you know the ball will come through quicker and make it harder for the attackers to reach the ball.

What are the characteristics required for a 'sweeper-keeper'?

I think that you definitely have to be brave to do this. You have to be prepared to make mistakes because you're not always going to get the call right.

Aside from being brave, you have to be tactically aware of each player and team you're up against, not only in the starting 11 but players that could come on as well. You have to know the strengths and weaknesses of all the players that could possibly be on the pitch.

From a physical point of view, it goes without saying that the quicker you are the quicker you'll be able to get to the ball, so it pays to keep working on this if you need to and also the larger you are means attackers have less of an angle to get past as well, if you do find yourself one-on-one.

Were there many times this season when the opposition have managed to expose your position?

I remember, specifically, Fulham away when Ross McCormack scored with an unbelievable finish from an angle where he lifted the ball over me.

I was in a good position and the ball was played over the top and out wide; it wasn't a ball I could come for so I started to get back into a position where I could deal with the shot. McCormack lifted the ball over me even though I had recovered into a good position. Sometimes this happens and it was an unbelievable goal...

McCormack himself said to me after that the staff at Fulham had told him that I'm really positive in my starting positions and to look for opportunities to expose that. On this occasion he scored when I was in a good recovery position but it was just a great finish.

COMMANDING YOUR AREA

EK - MB - DT - RL - ROD

Returning to Bristol City goalkeeper Richard O'Donnell, becoming an imperious and formidable force to be reckoned with as a goalkeeper is one of - if not the - most important aspects of the position. Let's find out a little bit more about what it means from a professional's perspective and how you can implement it moving

forward:

We've already touched a lot on starting position in the 'sweeper-keeper' feature, but how do you look to command your area from the early point of freekicks/corners?

I believe it's always important to come and help your team as much as you can. The key thing is being in a high/bold starting position, one that makes the free-kick/corner taker think "I'll have to swing this away a bit".

If they do that then great, it's easier to defend and the cross isn't as dangerous as it's further away from the goal. However, if they do still put it in and around you, your decision to try and make contact with the ball becomes an easier one.

Then comes the next decision and catch or punch/deflect away and we move forward from there...

What sort of things do you say to your back four/teammates during the match and how important do you view keeping this line of connection open?

I think that, when you're a goalkeeper, most of us feel we are natural leaders. Being vocal is a big part of a goalkeeper's game and this could be in a range of facets from instructions to encouragement to the occasional rollicking and so communication is obviously key.

Simple commands such as *"squeeze"* or *"get up"* are phases that are often used. Telling your full backs to *"tuck in"* and when crosses come and there's a decision to be made - it's either *"goalkeepers"* or *"away"*. These are probably the most common phases used.

The other side of communication is encouragement which I believe to be very important, especially if one of your team mates isn't having a great game or if someone makes a good tackle, plays a good ball etc.

It can go a long way to helping certain types of players if you've given them a vocal thumbs up. After playing with individuals for a while you get to understand what they respond to best.

Sometimes it might be a bit of a shouting at or sometimes it's positivity. Both aspects are vitally important.

Do you find that communication is important in helping you stay concentrated through the 90 minutes of game-play?

There's always going to be at least one game in a season where you have no saves to make. There'll be some where you have loads to do and you'll have an absolute worldie. Then there will be a game where you have nothing to do and all of a sudden you have to pop up with a save in the last minute to save a point, or three.

You have to be ready right until the last minute of a game even if you have nothing to do.

Personally, I do this through my communication: I'm always talking to the players in front of me and giving out instructions as I find this helps me stay switched on and, again, it makes things easier if you're getting the right information across and you're getting it across quick enough not just from the defence's perspective but also going forward as well.

GOALKEEPERS WILL OFTEN USE A RANGE OF COMMANDS TO HELP ORGANISE THEIR BACK LINE. HERE ARE SOME OF THE MORE COMMON TERMS:

"TUCK IN"
"SQUEEZE"
"PUSH UP"
"NO BOUNCE"
"NO CROSS/SHOT"
"SPLIT"
"GOALKEEPERS"
"AWAY"

IT'S IMPORTANT TO MAKE SURE YOUR TEAMMATES UNDERSTAND THESE, TOO, SO DISCUSS TOGETHER TO PREVENT ANY MISUNDERSTANDINGS!

CAPTAINING YOUR COUNTRY

EK - MB - DT - RL - ROD

Ask any captain and they'll tell you what an honour it is to lead your country. Many of us would like to see more goalkeepers as captains moving forward, but, regardless, Melissa Barbieri shares her experiences on captaining her Australian side to ASEAN Cup champions, among other achievements...

How did it come about for you to captain Australia?

I had been in the team for about 10 years and the previous captain retired so there was an opening in the ranks and, basically, our coach at the time put it to a vote to the players before he then went on to make the ultimate decision.

It transpires that the girls thought I was best suited to take the position which was really humbling and I was immensely honoured to captain my country, especially in the way we performed over the next couple of years.

The talent coming through at the time was great to see and it was brilliant that I could have an influence on them. Some say that we were maybe lacking that leadership or positive experience within the group but that's because we had an incredibly young team.

The majority of our players were 20 and under, so it was always just going to be a transitional phase but one that I am very pleased to have had the opportunity to influence the girls through, hopefully in a positive manner. To see how they're playing now and acting as professionals is great to see.

The group of girls that we had were – and still are! - really changing the face of Women's football. We lifted the ASEAN Cup straight off the mark in 2010 and to be able to say that I captained the first team to do that from Australia was such an honour.

Since then, we've had strong performances in the World Cup and things are really looking good for the Matildas moving forward.

What role would you have as captain? What were the sort of things you were saying to the players?

The players weren't at all used to the transition to being paid to play football, which was a big shock for a few of them I think so I certainly had to manage a lot of this and the changes of behaviour, mind-set and expectation because of it.

Social media, too, was a big thing for these girls. I was captain just as it was starting to

come to the forefront of the game, but it still took a good couple of years for the realisation that anything that's put on social media can be seen, and it can't then be unseen.

Especially with sponsors and the like, the brand image that these girls were creating was huge and it was so important that they were seen in the right light. At the end of the day, you want these sponsors to come back and spend more money on the clubs, players and country so it was my job as captain to just gently guide the girls in the correct direction.

Could it be a difficult role at times? What advice would you have for new-found captains?

I had to be the tough guy sometimes and I hope that they respected me for that. For example, I did have to lean on them a couple of times and say "look, that's not on - you just can't do that" and I suppose that's the very hard part of being a captain: you're not everyone's best friend.

Certainly, though, as long as you're always honest, truthful and straight-up with everyone about the way you go about things, you'll be respected for that, even if you do make mistakes, which all of us do from time to time.

THE MIND SET FOR SUCCESS

EK - MB - DT - RL - ROD

In the modern day, goalkeepers, coaches and managers seem to be recognising and valuing the importance of mental preparation more than ever before.

With Premier League appearances under his belt, as well as a very impressive penalty record, ex-Watford and Brentford goalkeeper Richard Lee gives his perspective and ideas on wiring our brains for that optimum level of performance.

> **AM I EATING CORRECTLY?**
>
> **WHAT IS MY MENTAL ATTITUDE?**
>
> **AM I EXCITED FOR THE GAME?**
>
> **HOW MUCH SLEEP HAVE I HAD?**
>
> **DO I EXPECT TO BE MOTM?**

Pre-match, how do you approach an impending game?

I personally talk about controlling the 'controllables' quite a lot. In my earlier years, I worried a lot about things that I couldn't control. I worried about what would happen if, for example, it was a wet and windy day and the ball came in from a cross, slipped through my hands because of the rain and found itself in the back of the net.

Now, naturally, if those are the sort of thoughts going through your head then you're going to be very nervous. So I talk a lot about controlling the things that you can control before the game...

These are all the sorts of things that mean you're more likely to perform well, if you can get them under control and act accordingly.

Additionally, I was very keen to avoid falling into the trap of having superstitions. They can limit your performance as they're not particularly in your control and therefore this can cause added anxiety as well, so it was never about superstitions but instead about what I could control and doing this to the best of my ability so that, come 15:00 on a Saturday, I was driven, focused and excited to play the game of football.

Could I guarantee that I was going to play well? No, of course not. Are you going to have a better chance of having a good game if you're built on sound preparation as oppose to superstition, though? Yes. Absolutely.

So that was definitely a big part of my preparation.

For me it's the difference between the good and the great. If you're not concerned about where you are mentally for a game then you're reliant on luck.

And, sure: you might have some great games. I'm sure all of us can relate to one or two times where we've felt terrible and had a great game and, likewise, where we've felt incredible and had a really poor game.

However, it is my firm belief that over the course of the season or a career, if you have awareness as to how you feel, then you are going to have so much more chance of playing a fantastic and successful career of football than if you're relying on luck from game-to-game to see you through it.

You look at the very best and they're all mentally very strong. One of the examples that I had close to me for a period of time was Ben Foster. He got so excited for a game of football, which was just how he was wired.

He was intrinsically wired to love being in front of a crowd and the centre of attention. He got a genuine buzz out of playing games of football and being the best he could be.

I've got no doubt at all now that this is the reason he's still playing at the top end of the Premier League and how he manages to come back from injury after injury, to a much bigger level than I necessarily have...

In a game, and under the huge pressures of playing professional football, how do you react to making a mistake?

It's difficult. You could make a mistake in the first minute and end up losing 1-0. You know that, even if you played incredibly well for the last 89 minutes of that game, you're going to be remembered for the goal you conceded.

Even the legends of the goalkeeping world, such as David Seaman, suffer from it too. It's incredible that a man who played so many games in the Premier League and internationally, with such an outstanding record, is remembered for the couple of times that he was lobbed...

It's largely down to the culture we're in, where people seem to focus on the negatives all of the time, almost 'looking' for a mistake. In order to counteract that as goalkeepers, we need to be so mentally strong. David Seaman is a great example of that, it's like mistakes wouldn't affect him – almost as if it was water off a duck's back.

For us to achieve that ourselves in the world of football, we really have to focus on how you choose to take in information:

Do you choose to take in the negativity from those mistakes and those around you?

or

Do you create your own reality, putting them under the rug, learning as much as you can about them and then getting up and moving on?

I think that's the fundamental basis of it all.

Communication is a big part of this. How can goalkeepers use it to encourage their teammates?

I've learnt so much about this recently that I wish I knew when I was younger!

Communication can make such a massive impact but as long as it's done in the right way. In order for it to have this impact, as a goalkeeper, you need to make sure that you're making calls with the right conviction and the connection with what is going on on the pitch.

The truth of the matter is that your defence is like your wall and you can be the eyes and ears for them – you can have a great deal of influence on how they perform and how they get on.

We've got great advantages as goalkeepers, being able to see everything that is going on within the pitch and therefore we can instruct our defenders accordingly.

When I was younger, I used to 'commentate'. The manager told me that I should be talking and I suppose there was a misunderstanding that this, on its own, was enough. I'd be saying the right things but it didn't matter; I wasn't saying it with conviction so the players weren't responding as required.

It's all about making sure you're the leader and the voice of authority on the pitch – you can stop so much happening without the ball coming anywhere near you.

If you are really strong with how you deal with your defensive units, you can keep clean sheet after clean sheet without people really noticing but you're performing so much better than the flamboyant goalkeepers that make save after save but maybe aren't the most effective in how they go about their performance.

Continuing on from this, goalkeepers often struggle with the confidence for a number of reasons... What advice would you give here?

The key thing with confidence is the awareness and realisation that nobody can give you confidence. It blew my mind when I was younger because I was always reliant on other people telling me that I'd done well and supporting me in this way.

When you realise that confidence is about you is the moment you can start to inspire and motivate yourself. It's not until this moment, where you totally believe that you can be a great goalkeeper, that you have the opportunity to become a great goalkeeper.

There aren't always going to be people around you to support and motivate you so it becomes so important that we – ourselves – can give that extra boost of confidence.

As soon as you start to understand that it's your thoughts that generate your feelings, you can start to dictate and direct yourself and your behaviour, giving that extra level of confidence and helping to perform to that higher level in football or whatever else it may be.

Transition slightly here, how important is it to retain concentration across the 90 minutes of game time?

I think that it's all about levels of concentration. For example, when we had a corner, I knew that I might have a few seconds to relax, switch off, whatever it might be. At the end of the day, can anyone concentrate for 90 minutes 100%? Maybe, maybe not.

But, certainly, I think it can be a considerable help when you are aware as to when you need to be concentrating and when you have the opportunity to take your foot off the gas for a few seconds.

Ultimately, in a game of football, you may only touch the ball 30 or 40 times over 90 minutes, but for those short periods where you are called into action, you need to be fully prepared and ready.

It may be that all of a sudden a long ball is lumped through and the attacker happens to be one-on-one; you have the decision to make about whether you come or whether you stay. I always liken it to a game of chess: you always need to be aware and tuned in as to what could follow next, one or two steps ahead of the actual game.

You've always dealt quite well with penalties through your career... How did you approach penalties to be so successful in this manner?

My belief on penalties was very simple: make a decision and then commit to that decision.

Most of the time, the striker should score... They've got three main decisions (left, right or centre) so once you've made your decision then absolutely go all out.

Unless it's a superb penalty right in the corner, you've got a really good chance of making the save.

Also, you can use the mind-set of "if I go the right way I expect to save this penalty" which will help you create an imposing figure and strong body language in the goal, ultimately helping you to get in the mind of the attacker.

Every penalty situation I entered was with the mantra "I expect to save this ball, if you go the way I think you will', regardless of whether I had scored or conceded the last five - each penalty was a unique situation.

If we break it down, we can probably see it in 4 or 5 steps:

1) Assess what type of player am I up against? Is it a centre-half likely to punt it down the middle? A winger who might come back across himself?

2) Based on this, which way am I going to dive?

3) Make sure that I look imposing and imperious in the goal, knowing the pressure is on the striker.

4) Dive full out and try to make the save!

Finally, what techniques specifically have you come across for enhancing success through psychology and harnessing your mind?

One of the biggest aids for me personally, and something that I think has the power to make huge differences to the lives of all of us, is neuro-linguistic programming. Basically, as the name suggests, it uses language to programme the mind.

We have to understand that a lot of what goes through our minds we create: people have 50,000 thoughts one day and 45,000 of the same thoughts the next. This means that we are creatures of habit.

How we're wired, how we operate, if you like, is a direct output of the results we're going to get. Now, you can imagine for football that this is hugely powerful.

A lot of the insecurity and self-doubt that I previously had was transferred through positive thoughts and I went on to win all 4 Player of the Year awards at Brentford, as well as winning the captaincy, and I've got no doubt that it was the mental preparation I did that hugely contributed to that.

It didn't happen overnight, certainly, but it definitely had a profound impact on my game and life.

As far as getting people into NLP, I would recommend taking a look at some of the online courses available, as well as also starting to think about the personal development side of things, too, as that can be very fundamental to improving and enhancing performance.

There's actually an app called 'Blinkist', which I have no affiliation with. It reduces every personal development book into a 15 minute audio book or summary and is really good for taking the key messages out of books, without necessarily having to read the whole thing.

A lot of people now are starting to realise that success and achievement don't come by accident: you have to improve something intrinsically to bring about some kind of extrinsic reward.

The personal development that you do will have a huge influence on all aspects of your life, whether that be your relationships, your career (and your football beyond that) or even just the way you see yourself – I can't speak highly enough of the importance of personal development.

Every single person on this planet needs and requires personal development to grow and achieve the things that they want to achieve.

You can find out more about Rich's approach to psychology through football with his performance agency, www.refuelperformance.com **and his personal website at** www.dickielee.com. **His GKIcon franshise can also be found online, too.**

SCIENCE OF GOALKEEPING

The physical part of goalkeeping is one that continues to grow. In the modern day, goalkeepers across the world are looking for that extra 1% to take them to the top of their game and, often, one big way in which this is realised is through the physical side of the game. We speak to Oxford United's Lead Sports Scientist Scott Daly about how goalkeepers can best prepare for impending fixtures as well as the right things to eat, the importance of sleep and much more!

THE BODY IN DEVELOPMENT

SCOTT DALY

For the first in our series of features with OUFC Sports Scientist Scott Daly, we look at the effects of heavy and intense work on growing adolescents, as well as the ideal ways to teach primary movements and hand-eye coordination.

We hear a lot about 'stunted' growth harming long-term development of athletes. What's your opinion on this?

Movement and resistance training supports long-term athletic development. I don't really think it's a case of my opinion anymore...

So much research has been done that now it's more like science, it's basically fact.

But, that being said, when you've got a kid who's all of a sudden had a massive growth spurt, and they become incredibly uncoordinated and generally aren't moving the way they were before, their movements aren't so efficient and, all of a sudden, the day-to-day training that they were doing before is becoming incredibly more demanding.

It's putting loads more stress on their joints and muscles, which aren't working in coordination and efficiently.

And, if you keep working this child with a large load and lots of work, they're just going to break down and their body is not going to get used to the changes that have happened.

How can we mitigate the risks of stunted growth?

One way to avoid this is to instead teach them primary movements through strength training. Things like how to squat, how to jump, how to land, single leg stability, single leg reactivity are all very helpful.

These are all just movements that kids were doing 10 or 15 years ago when they were climbing games and playing loads of sport.

Look at the younger generation now, though, and it might make me sound old for someone who's only 28!, but they're playing computer games, sitting inside and generally not learning and using as much of these primary movements as before.

It's important as a strength and conditioning coach to recognise this aspect and not load them up with football, football, football, as overuse injuries will most likely occur.

There are loads of things we can do like using other sports such as gymnastics, basketball and maybe some time in the gym, but the bottom line is to keep them moving.

Keep them using as many different muscles and keep them learning how to coordinate their body efficiently whilst they're going through that awkward adolescent period.

So should we not be loading children at all?

As long as they're moving well, you can load. Of course, I'm not saying we should be really pushing the kids and looking for growth of muscles but you can develop strength through body weight exercises.

Initially, gaining strength might be learning to do something like a squat but in a really efficient body pattern, thus becoming stronger at that movement. Once they're proficient at it, then there's no issue with getting some weight working with them too.

Strength training is definitely beneficial, as long as it's at the right time and done in the right way.

What benefits do you create from encouraging a multi-sport approach?

You're creating an all-round athlete. Especially as a goalkeeper, the hand-eye coordination aspect is massive. It also helps to develop them as a person because you're giving them different experiences, cultures and personalities through sports that can really help you develop the athlete further.

I say athlete because, at the end of the day, that is the main message: it's about developing the athlete, not the footballer or goalkeeper. Doing multi-sport is absolutely crucial to that.

You can find out more about Scott's own work, including his personal training business based in Berkhamsted, at www.dalyperformance.wordpress.com.

STRENGTH AND CONDITIONING

SCOTT DALY

Strength and conditioning is a huge part of any goalkeeper's game. No matter what level you're playing at, it gives goalkeepers the potential to reach new heights (literally!) as well as a plethora of other benefits for your development as an athlete and in your health in general.

How can you motivate a goal goalkeeper to increase strength and fitness?

In terms of fitness on the pitch, working hard in training will take care of that and it should really look after itself. An area that I would like to see improve in football is the redirection of players' attention towards the strength side of the game.

We see players all the time pulling up with hamstring, groin and overuse injuries because they – essentially – can't deal with the loads over a period of time.

We can reduce overuse injuries by being strong because the weight you're putting on yourself is comparatively less as your muscles are able to deal with it to a better degree.

From the perspective of effective strength, though, thinking about things like efficiency and capability in movement is massively important...

If you're a stronger athlete you're going to be a more powerful and agile goalkeeper; being strong is a foundation to all athletic development.

If you haven't got strength, the other areas of your development are going to lack. Simple things like recognising that in sprinting or high-level jumping each leg can be exposed to forces 10 times greater than body weight and that, if you're strong, you're going to be able to deal with this much more efficiently.

What are the most important areas for a goalkeeper to be working on?

Again, strength is all encompassing. If you're strong on two legs, you can get into these different positions and you'll be strong through a range of movements.

It can prove vitally helpful in things like commanding your box and area, as well as coming to claim crosses: being strong allows you to make contact and not to be worried about being thrown over by the opposition.

Being agile, also, is essential for a goalkeeper. Essentially, it is the ability to shift your centre of mass. It's not about moving your feet incredibly quickly, like you might see on some 'experts' Instagram page, that's called having really quick feet!

I might have feet that are incredibly useful if I'm an Irish dancer, but it's not necessarily too good for a goalkeeper...

You want to be able to move your whole body in multiple directions, with force and speed, and strength allows you to increase your power which, in turn, will increase your agility.

From a science perspective how can we look at the nature of goalkeeping?

The primary movements in goalkeeping - when a goalkeeper is called into action - are actions very high in speed and intensity.

The energy system mostly utilised is the ATP and Phosphocreatine system (ATP-PC), also known as the Phosphagen system. It is immediate and functions in the absence of oxygen.

It allows for approximately 12 seconds of intense work and is replenished after 3-5 minutes once exhausted.

The aerobic system plays a large role in the replenishing of ATP. Increased aerobic capacity allows for greater oxygen flow to working muscles, via mitochondria in blood, and therefore increased recovery between bouts of exercise.

A little too heavy for me! How do we go about conditioning goalkeepers best?

You want to start off with things as general as possible, maybe looking at one specific movement or skill. Once you're happy with that, you can make this into a situation or exercise where things are really multi-directional. This will build up that skill further.

If you're satisfied with this level, you can start to move it into the real reactive game-scenarios, where the goalkeeper doesn't necessarily know what will happen next.

Don't do it the other way around. Don't think: I'm a goalkeeper now, so I'm going to work on this particular detail. Instead, work on the basics and get a really solid basis as a foundation before then moving on to the specifics as time goes on.

How do you set goals for your players?

We base our goals on our testing. We will look at the players we've got, where some will be generally weaker than others, without it being towards one particular leg, for example.

Quite simply, we'll just let them know that we need to get them stronger and more robust.

For other players, we might find that one leg is slightly stronger than the other in some regard. What we need to do with these is to balance it up a bit, obviously... For sure, we target based on what the players are good at and what they need to improve.

You should definitely keep working on the things that you're good at in order to become excellent at it and then – over time – a master at it.

The things you're not so good at you should try to move from poor to average and then on to good eventually.

A SPORTING LIFESTYLE...

SCOTT DALY

The goalkeeper's lifestyle is imperative to his performance in the modern game. Whether it be the food you're eating or the amount of sleep you're getting, it all adds up and will ultimately help you reach that next level of performance, development and recovery:

What is the importance of diet, especially in the modern era of football?

I think that diet is massively important. The demands of the game now are huge, with everything from the training to the fixture schedules, which are borderline ridiculous sometimes...

Therefore, if you're not eating the right foods, you're not going to recover between sessions and you'll be going into sessions under-recovered and under-prepared.

I don't think fitness really comes into it in the professional season. When you get to the match time, I don't ever think that players are unfit. Instead, they can often be a little bit stale, lacking in freshness, and just not ready to play the game to the best of their potential.

In which case, what are the best foods that players should be eating?

I think this is something really simple that people try to overcomplicate. Eat fresh foods: vegetables, meat and whole, good sources of carbohydrates.

Things like sweet potato, quinoa and rice, with their slow-release energy, will last you all day if you have them the morning of a game or the night before. If you have something like pasta, or a loaf of bread, though, you'll get a quick release of energy but by the time you get to the game you might actually get an energy slump as you get to the other side of it.

The same applies to a bar of chocolate: your sugar levels will rise, and then crash right back down and you'll end up feeling a little bit tired and maybe lethargic.

As a goalkeeper, what are the best things to be having pre-match?

The demands of a goalkeeper are very different to the demands of an outfield player. Ensuring that you're fuelled to perform is essential, of course, but you could be working really intensely for 10 or 20 seconds at a time and then you may well have a long rest.

Therefore, you probably won't need large stores of carbohydrates to get you through the game.

The sources of food still remain the same, for sure, but it may be that the quantities in which they are consumed are less.

From a fluids perspective, we give the guys electrolyte tablets, which are basically salts dissolved into water, replenishing the lost salts in the body. It's important to remember that you can over hydrate so, if you're drinking loads of water, it's important to think about potentially putting some squash in it to balance out the concentration.

If it's just all water, you'll find yourself having to go to the toilet all the time and you're actually dehydrating yourself in the process! Having that little bit of salt in the liquid will help you retain it better.

How does sleep impact on recovery for an athlete?

Sleep, in my opinion, is the most important aspect of recovery: if you're not sleeping, you're not recovering. There are studies out there to show that, at a professional level, if you get less than about 7.5/8 hours sleep a night, you're 1.5 times more likely to get injured.

And, if this applies at a professional level, it almost certainly applies to the likes of the academy players and others where they're playing and training 3 or 4 times a week.

There are a variety of things which will influence your quality and quantity of sleep. Thins like poor food choices late at night and during the day will impact your sleep, especially with foods high in saturated fats because an overly fatty diet will lead to a more fragmented and therefore less effective sleep.

Also, looking at your phone before you go to bed will reduce the quality of your sleep, as it releases blue light which supresses melatonin levels.

Melatonin is responsible for making you feel sleepy at the end of the day so this can seriously mess with your sleeping pattern.

Ideally, you don't want any electronics in the room, although I do understand that this might be difficult in the modern world... Many people have their phone as their alarm clock, at the end of the day!

THE WARM UP & COOL DOWN

SCOTT DALY

The warmup and cool down is a fundamental part of any goalkeepers match preparation and recovery. Over his years of experience and applying theory from the world of science, Scott tells us the best way to make sure you're warmed up as effectively as possible:

How would you put together a specialised goalkeeper warmup?

I think that I'd treat it exactly the same as an outfield player, in the sense that anything he will be doing in the game, he should be doing in the warmup.

I'm not saying the exercises will be the same as an outfield player, but if he's going to have to take a cross in the game he should come and be taking a cross in the warmup, too.

Of course, you want to gradually introduce them to all these things. One simple technique we use to do this is called RAMP:

**R – RAISE HEART RATE
A – ACTIVATE MUSCLES
M – MOBILISE JOINTS
P – POTENTIATE**

This principle applies to anything, such as a standard training session, too. Most coaches do it, probably without realising: they will most likely start with a little bit of general movement before doing some basic handling work or taking some crosses and then, over time, gradually increasing the intensity of the work. By the very end of the warmup the goalkeeper is doing things like taking shots in more match-specific situations.

Does the same apply to the cool down?

A cool down for me can sometimes be overemphasised, in my opinion. Especially after intense exercise, we're going out there and stretching muscles which are already torn and damaged because you've had a really good and intense game of football.

Is stretching a torn muscle the best thing to be doing? Possibly not. A cool down might be something like a little gentle walk, reducing the heart rate gradually and maybe some mobility work, too, to restore range of motion to the joints.

For me, though, the real cool down is coming in, having the right recovery food, drinks or whatever else it may be and then getting a sufficient amount of sleep – those are my most vital things to any cool down.

#FUTSAL FEVER

Whether it be because of the abundant viral futsal videos, the fast-paced nature of the game or the growing globalisation of all sports, futsal is one that is certainly beginning to take off in the UK and doing so at a great rate. Encompassing a big emphasis on distribution, sharp reflexes and incredible flexibility, the goalkeeper's game is definitely not an easy one. But this is part of the reason it is so attractive to goalkeepers across the country, here are a couple of big names to share more...!

TE   **Tony Elliott** - As featured previously, former England Fustal Goalkeeper Coach. Tony has a wealth of experience in coaching different aspects of the footballing game, from futsal to disability football, such as the England blind squads with sighted goalkeepers.

TD   **Thomas Dennis** - England International Futsal Goalkeeper for the senior team. Alongside this, Tom also studied at Loughborough university and is now in full-time work alongside his international career - an interesting combination and one we'll be taking a good look at!

DT   **Dean Thornton** - QPR Lead Academy Goalkeeping Coach and former England Futsal International. Dean's goalkeeping career spanned a number of football clubs, such as Wycombe Wanderers, before moving into coaching.

JOURNEYING INTO FUTSAL

TE · TD · DT

Futsal is an infamously fast-paced game, where the position of the goalkeeper is pivotal. No matter what the score or situation, the goalkeeper will always have work to do and this is one of the reasons it is quite so attractive to goalkeepers through the UK, as England international goalkeepers Tom Dennis and Dean Thornton explain, as well as former national goalkeeper coach Tony Elliot:

When did you first become interested in futsal, how did you get into it and who did you first play for?

I only came across futsal through my football club, St Andrews FC. The managers at the club liked the idea of futsal and thought it would help our all-round football game as well as using it as a fitness tool.

It was new to all of us so it was a case of learning as we went along and seeing what would work and what we found useful to us.

We were always a pretty successful side at futsal which always helps, reaching the national semi-finals as a minimum every year, and that helps to maximise your enjoyment but it was the fast pace of the game and that, as a goalkeeper, no matter how much you are dominating a game, in futsal you will always have things to do in a game that really had

me hooked.

Everything about futsal seemed to interest me: the fact it was so fast-paced, always involved the goalkeeper and there wasn't such a big emphasis on how tall you were as a goalkeeper.

What aspect of futsal do you enjoy most?

I have always been a goalkeeper but liked to play football from the back and get involved with the play myself and this is what drew my interest to futsal in a big way.

Although in futsal the goalkeeper can only receive one back pass during one phase of play, there is also the 'fly goalkeeper' tactic. This is where the goalkeeper effectively becomes an extra outfield player and crosses the halfway line.

I used to enjoy this as our set pieces at St Andrews used to involve this a lot and led to me scoring a few goals (which obviously doesn't happen very often as a goalkeeper!!).

At what age did you begin to receive specialist goalkeeper coaching?

I had no specialised futsal goalkeeper training until I was called up to the England

U19 setup...

It was very rare to find any sort of futsal goalkeeper training around at that time. Fortunately, now there are a few goalkeeper coaches out there who are running workshops and training sessions, specific for futsal and these are a huge help.

Up until the stage of getting coaching, it was always just playing off instinct and seeing what worked best for me. I was always a goalkeeper who would use my feet to save a shot if it felt right to do so and I was never afraid to use unconventional saves to keep the ball out the net.

When I started to move towards playing futsal more seriously, I noticed this was now becoming more apparent in the professional football game.

The likes of De Gea and Hugo Lloris coming to the Premier League has helped the public perception that it isn't against any sort of rule that you have to use your hands to save a goal - you can use any part of your body as long as it does the job of stopping the ball!

From the goalkeeper's perspective, what are the important aspects of a futsal coach?

The main thing I look for in a goalkeeper coach in futsal is that they relate almost everything to a game situation. There are times where we use different equipment (volleyballs, tennis balls, bibs, weights etc), however everything will be linked to a game situation so I never felt as though I was doing practices for the sake of just training.

What can young goalkeepers be doing to improve and get into the idea of futsal a bit more?

Now the game has grown a lot more, young goalkeepers can just search for futsal specific goalkeeper drills online and there will be plenty which come up. A few videos of goalkeepers abroad have made it viral as the training drills for futsal are very easy on the eye and very explosive so people do like to watch a futsal goalkeeper at work.

You can be looking at things like mastering the basics of the 'K' shape, made famous by Peter Schmeichel, the 'splits' to enable the goalkeeper to save shots which are low and close range (not giving enough time for the conventional dive). The younger you get the training the better as this is when the body is most flexible.

You're now working full time whilst playing for the England Senior team... How do you manage both working and training at the same time?

This is the extremely difficult side of English futsal. There are very few chances currently to become professional so the majority of the squad are amateur as I am. It can become incredibly hard at times.

For example, in October, we began our World Cup qualifying campaign...

We made it into the main qualifying round for the first time in our young national history and this took up a lot of time between the two rounds and with warmup games and training camps squeezed in, too. I think I can recall only being at home for two or three weekends through the month of October up until Christmas!

This, in itself, brings a lot of sacrifices that I have had to make in order to maintain where I am and try to improve myself as much as possible.

I am exceptionally lucky to have a very understandable family and girlfriend who are willing to support me in every possible way and happy to give up their time in order for

me to play for my country - something that I have dreamt about since I was a young boy.

Playing futsal for England may not be the playing for England which I dreamt of but the feeling I get when playing for my country, walking out to the national anthem, is still something that I am extremely proud of and makes every one of the sacrifices worth it.

The lack of facilities for futsal is another sticking point: the times of training sessions can be very late due to the few number of sports halls that have futsal goals and the adequate court dimensions. This leads to the training sessions starting and finishing quite late at night and, taking into consideration the travel time to get to and from training, it can get very late indeed.

This makes the strain of training harder as it starts to affect the day to day pressures of work due to the nature of training.

Also, as we are only amateur, there is nobody there to help us look after ourselves with our diets and training schedules - it's up to us to make sure that we are fit enough to be playing to an international standard.

Now, this can be very difficult as it could involve training on top of our club sessions to make sure we are the top level we can be so our social time really starts to become very narrow and that's where it is important to have that supporting family.

As an England squad, we do not get to meet up as often as we would like. This is mainly due to the fact that not many of us are professional and there is only so much time that you can take off work and from your family before it starts to become unrealistic.

On average, we will meet up around once every couple of months for a 4-day camp and train two or three times a day. However, in the build up to a major tournament this can become a much more regular occurrence.

In a perfect world I would love to be playing futsal professionally in 5 years' time. I get so much more satisfaction from playing and winning in futsal rather than football but that is just a personal opinion of mine.

I think that with wider exposure of the game and with the right people backing the game then it could really take off.

For all the goalkeeper conferences and futsal taster sessions that I have been involved in, I am yet to see one football coach that doesn't see a benefit to take back to their football team. This needs, though, to stop being a theory and be put into practice instead.

I think that, once this is all in place and futsal gets the exposure that I believe it deserves in this country, the game could really take off and who knows where this could possibly take us.

I am extremely excited and passionate about this and truly believe that every kid whether in school or at a club should be exposed to

futsal to help improve their game.

TONY ELLIOTT

From a very early age I think that I was probably destined to be a goalkeeper.

My dad used to run a Sunday League team and from the age of 7 or 8 – back in the day when it was allowed! – I used to train with the men. It was quite a tough initiation to goalkeeping, but many quickly realised I had a natural talent to throwing myself around, especially as working with grown men at that stage was very difficult to keep up with.

I went on to play local football and was seen as quite a late developer. At the age of about 13, scouts started to come and watch me from a variety of different clubs through my local area of the Midlands and beyond.

I had the choice of a lot of big clubs at the time (the likes of Aston Villa, Tottenham and Notts Forest) but I went, in the end, for my boyhood team Birmingham City – it was always my dream to play for them one day.

When I turned 16, I was selected for the FA's national schoolboy squad and this involved spending two years living at Lilleshall, the England camp at the time, where we were the guinea pigs for the FA as the first 25 boys selected on a new regime that would go on to continue until the year 2000.

It was a fantastic honour to be selected and, if the opportunity was there again, I'd do it in an instant! The experience was unbelievable. We spent two years learning our trade and playing for England, as fortunately I was also selected for England schoolboys, which meant I managed to play at Wembley a couple of times, too...

All of these experiences were a fantastic learning curve for me, and taught me a lot about being a person as well as a footballer

– they're a large part of the person you see before you today.

What about your professional career... Could you give us any stats from that?

I played professionally, then, signing pro at Birmingham when I was 17. I went on to play until I was 30, after being forced into retirement, racking up around 250 appearances as a goalkeeper but it was the injuries that finished me off.

I always thought I was very fit, I've looked after myself and when you get to 30 you normally think as a goalkeeper you've still got 10 years left in you, especially in the modern game, so it was a bit of a shame that I was derailed by injuries to that extent.

Upon retiring, how did you make the move into coaching?

There wasn't any coaching work at the time I retired, so I actually ended up stacking shelves at Morrisons for about 6 months whilst I got my coaching badges. After completing my badges, my first step was getting in contact with the Lancashire FA, who offered me some work with their venues across the North.

This was a bit of a trek for me but it set me off on the coaching pathway, being the only option open to me at the time, and I was able to develop my coaching from there.

It was certainly a difficult period because I was still working at Morrisons – I had a family to think about and to feed.

There is obviously a big difference between the wage of a professional footballer, and the trimmings and extras that come with that, compared to working in a supermarket, so pride soon went out the window and I just did what I had to do to support my family and try to get back on the coaching ladder.

Again, though, I come back to it: it was a great learning lesson because it makes you realise just how fortunate we are to be around and involved in football.
I vowed in the moment I left Morrisons that I'd never be out of football again and, fortunately, to this day, that has managed to ring true...

I've always been involved in the game and hopefully that will continue for some time.

After I'd left Morrisons, I actually set up my own goalkeeping school locally. At two or three different venues each week, we'd have goalkeepers down and offer them some good quality coaching, which there wasn't much of at the time.

Over time, Roddy Collins, someone that I knew quite well, got the full-time manager job at Carlisle United and he offered me a full-time position there, overseeing all the goalkeeper's schedules and working with the backroom staff.

I was there for around three seasons which was a really good chance to get into the senior coaching environment.

They were in League Two at the time but they had a new backer and there was a lot of money coming into the club which was great because I was looked after, had a full-time position and was well in the process of making something at Carlisle.

As always in football, though, things were destined to change at little notice and the manager got the sack, leaving me out of the game for a little while more.

Fortunately, my goalkeeper school was doing well so I was able to walk back into that to support me, and basically I just gave that all of my time for the next couple of years.

So what was the next step from here?

We had a lot of goalkeepers develop and get picked up by professional clubs through the goalkeeper school and it was also building me up a profile of a reputable coach in the area.

This really stepped up when I had a young

goalkeeper, a very talented young lad, who'd been with us for a couple of years.

I was never one for pushing goalkeepers into professional clubs, though, as I'm a firm believer in that, if you're good enough, you'll be picked up or spotted anyway – it's my job to help develop the goalkeepers as their coach, not necessarily to be their agent.

This young goalkeeper was playing for the county at the time. He had a game with a couple of scouts from Liverpool and Manchester United watching and, luckily for me, the boy had a fantastic game and both clubs contacted the parents, wanting the boy to go for trials.

The question both of them were asked was "who has been working with your son?" and obviously my name was then thrown onto the table.

Within the space of about 48 hours, I had phone calls with both of them asking me to meet them and eventually to run and initiate goalkeeping development centres outside of their catchment areas, with the idea that we could develop goalkeepers who maybe were good enough over time to move into the academy.

This was all about an opportunity for me to produce goalkeepers moving towards the next level, but more than that it was just a massive honour to have, arguably, the two biggest clubs in English football come after me and it was quite a decision for me to eventually make!

I went for Liverpool in the end, a bit of a gut feeling among other reasons, and it was one of the best decisions I ever made...

The aim, over all of the meetings we had, was to develop one goalkeeper who would make the step up to the academy over the first three years of the program, to sign full-time.

In the first year we found three, which really got me noticed from within the club and within 18 months I was asked to leave the development centre to someone else and instead go and work with the signed

goalkeepers at the club on a regular basis and help out the head of goalkeeping there.

Over time, this stepped up and I was asked to come in more and more, before being heavily involved in their international soccer schools. By the time I'd left, I was spending a lot of the summers abroad, leading a group of staff within the international soccer schools.

This was when the move into the world of futsal occurred, how did this transpire?

The head coach of the England Futsal team at the time, Graham Dell, was good friends with a couple of the coaches in the Liverpool Academy setup and also in the market for a new goalkeeper coach.

He wanted to take the sport in a new direction and my name was thrown into the mix, so Graham contacted me and offered me the opportunity to go down and meet the squad.

Within the first 10 minutes, I absolutely fell in love with the game of futsal.

Graham phoned me the next day to ask what I thought... I told him I loved it and he offered me a job! Nine years later, I am still at it and it has been an unbelievable experience to drive the program as I had to, as there were no specialist goalkeeper coaches at the time, so I'm very proud of the specialism that I had to work very hard to create.

When I first came into it, there was no education or ready-made syllabus for me to work from, the game was very much raw, and so I had to start with a blank canvas and work on some self-taught ideas to see where they'd take the game.

I immersed myself in the sport, looking, listening and understanding at every opportunity I had and really just trying to get to grips with what the futsal goalkeeper actually was and how to best coach it.

I kind of had to throw the goalkeeping manual out the window because it's a very different game and we were constantly working to transform natural football goalkeepers into futsal players - there were no futsal goalkeepers at the time!

I'd never profess to being an expert in the game, certainly not, but I think after nine years of analysing how goalkeepers play, building up an ideal skillset for a coach and the player, I'm probably as near to that as we get in this country at the minute, although there's certainly still an awful lot to learn.

It was an incredible experience; I had the opportunity to travel around the world and I would wholly recommend it to any goalkeeper.

DEAN THORNTON

How did you get into futsal?

The futsal was a weird one, actually. I was doing my first professional year at Wycombe and was out on loan at Banbury at the time. I then got an email through from the club to say that I'd been called up for the England squad. It was about 2007, then, and I'd never heard of the game at all.

I spoke to a few people and they told me it was beach football, so I was absolutely buzzing! I then got another email through about the training camp and they said that it would be located at Lilleshall.

Immediately, I was thinking that there aren't too many beaches in Birmingham...

So I travelled to Lilleshall with a group of about 20 players and 3 or 4 goalkeepers. The nucleus of the squad was already in place and I was chatting to them about how they'd got on so far. It was something along the lines of "we've played 20 games and lost all 20". Already, at this point, I was starting to ask some questions!

We played the game, though, and I absolutely loved it. Graham Dell was the manager at the time and he invited me along to Turkey after my first training session. Before I knew it, I was told that I was starting the first match. It took me back a bit, but I ended up being No1 for about three years, working with a variety of different goalkeepers over the time period.

THE FUTSAL GOALKEEPER

TE - TD - DT

They say it takes a special breed to be a goalkeeper. It takes an even more specific skillset to hold the fort in futsal, though, with pin-point accuracy a must and the ability to react to shots at point-blank range absolutely vital. Tony Elliott, once more, fills us in on the details:

How important is the goalkeeping position on the futsal court?

I'm a firm believer that the goalkeeper is the most important player on the futsal pitch (even if I am saying that with a slight bias!).

Obviously they're the first line of attack, with the ability to start counter-attacking movements on a regular basis, but they also have a huge job defensively due to the number of attacking phases within a game of futsal and therefore the sheer number of opportunities they have to keep the ball out of the goal.

What are the big differences between futsal and football?

The nature of the game obviously makes a huge difference. Things like the court size, the surface, the size of the goals and the weight of the ball all add to the dynamics of

the game for a goalkeeper.

For example, there doesn't tend to be as much diving as in conventional football, as the goalkeeper uses their feet a lot more, whilst techniques such as the lateral split are more economical and efficient for the goalkeeper and also save the pain of consistently diving on a hard surface which does take its toll.

The ball, also, as aforementioned, is heavier and slightly smaller which – combined with the speed and nature of the game – means that goalkeepers tend not to catch a lot, instead opting to deflect, parry or push the ball away to safety.

Obviously they will secure the ball if they can, because then we can look to starting a counter attack, but this is not a common practice.

Are there many cross-overs between the two sports?

There are definitely some transferable elements in the skillset; the flavour of the month is the 1v1 'cross technique', as we call it in futsal. This utilises all four limbs to cover the goal and, whilst this may be new in mainstream goalkeeping, it's been a

technique used by futsal goalkeepers for decades gone-by.

I actually delivered this particular technique on the FA Goalkeeper Conference 4 years ago, with the English futsal goalkeepers at the time... You could maybe say that the 400 people who saw and were blown away by the day have taken that into mainstream football.

If that is the case, then I'm very proud of that and we've added to the skillset of many, many football goalkeepers...

Of course, we'll never know directly, but it would fit in well with the timelines if this was, potentially, one of the catalysts.

I think the other thing that is very prevalent in futsal is distribution.

The importance of accuracy in futsal cannot be overstated, as a goalkeeper's ability to drop the ball at the feet of a teammate can be the start of a counter-attack or at least possession, whereas if this delivery is poor you lose possession again and suddenly you're on the back foot.

Especially with futsal, because everything happens quicker, you can literally go from having possession one second, to losing it the next and a few seconds later having

conceded a goal. In football, there is generally more of a build up but in futsal it happens in a snap second so poor distribution can really hold you back.

What are the qualities that a futsal goalkeeper needs?

The goalkeeper has to be able to split and half split (both sides - left and right) as well as have the core strength and agility to pop up and be back in the action immediately.

Also, as much as we can, you have to be able play with both feet due to the pressure in the tight space of the court with attackers constantly breathing down your throat - the multifunctional aspect is absolutely vital.

Looking at reflexes, as a coach, I'll use all sorts of different balls with different weights and sizes, to give different context to the ball and ensuring it's travelling at different heights, speeds and trajectories because the goalkeepers don't get that second in-game to think about what they're doing.

If the ball is 6-metres out and being toe-poked at you, with no back lift, then you've got no more than a split-second to react and make the save.

In this case does it come down to anticipation?

This is an interesting one because sometimes it's important to anticipate but if you do this too early or in the wrong way you're certainly leaving yourself exposed.

I think this is something we're starting to see more and more in mainstream football these days. One or two goalkeepers have been going too early with things like the block and the ball is being lifted over them or passed under them.

There's a place for everything, but the skill involved is being able to correctly execute the right decision at the right time... aka knowing when to use the block and when you're best standing up, for example.

The great thing for me recently has been that we've had a massive amount of interest from the professional game, interested in having me down to do a workshop or look at their goalkeepers.

The reason this is, though, is because they've seen the end product: the goalkeeper making the spread or the block. What they maybe don't understand is the process that goes before this... How do we move away from the idea of traditional 1v1s as they've been taught and instead move towards changing this?

The first one for me who did this really well was Pepe Reina. You look at him and he must have played some futsal in his younger years.

Forgive me if I'm wrong, but he will have had influence as to how that use that technique and he is, in my view, the first foreign influence to bring it to the English game and then obviously it's picked up from there.

If you haven't had it in your skillset since you were a youngster, you can't just turn around and say I'm going to do that, because there's a process and learning curve to it; you'll get found out.

Is height important in futsal?

No, in short. You watch futsal competitions across the world and you'll see all different shapes and size of goalkeepers. You'll see some that are 6"4 or so, basically taller than the goal, and then others who are 5"10 and very dynamic, fast, speedy and still doing a very good job.

One of the reasons for this is in terms of the game: mainstream football has a focus not just on covering the goal but also on defending crosses.

Well, immediately there are two things there with futsal that don't apply. You're only defending a 3x2m goal, which is easier for a smaller goalkeeper to cover, and there are, of course, no high crosses coming in.

Obviously, when you are taller, it'll help you in terms of the splits as you'll have a further reach and be able to make areas further across your goal.

Where the shorter goalkeeper might have to make a lateral movement first to get closer to source, a tall goalkeeper can minimise these extra movements by going straight down. This is going very deeply into the game and the mechanics of it. Again, it's all about awareness and perception.

What kind of things are in the Futsal Talent ID profile?

We understand with English futsal at present that we're always going to be transforming football goalkeepers into futsal goalkeepers, so that obviously changes things a little bit.

The athleticism and flexibility is definitely a big one, but we put to that as well having some composure and a little bit of calmness in game, as well as spot-on distribution, which is crucially important.

We use the four corners model massively, but we always throw the tactical side of futsal into the technical corner too, given its importance in the game and the fact that the goalkeeper can have such a big influence on the management of the game. I think it's also imperative to talk about the psychological side of things and the social corner too, both as aforementioned.

Goalkeepers aren't always going to tick every box, but if they do tick enough boxes then we will have the opportunity and ability to work with and mould these goalkeepers into players that are fit for international futsal.

TOP 5 FUTSAL GK ATTRIBUTES

TE - TD - DT

Futsal, as we've already seen, is a game with some thoroughly interesting dynamics that take it away from the game of football as we know it. Here's current England goalkeeper Thomas Dennis on the most important skills a Futsal goalkeeper must have to succeed in the game:

1) FLEXIBILITY

Due to the pace of the game, there are numerous times at which you do not find yourself in the perfect set position as a platform to save the shot. As a futsal goalkeeper, you must be able to adapt to these situations and find a way to get some part of the body to the ball to make the save.

One of the basics of futsal goalkeeping, therefore, is being able to perform the 'splits' save. This is a tool which we use when the ball is travelling at a fast speed either across the floor or very low.

You quite often see the difficulties football goalkeepers have when the ball is in the area around the lower feet at around hip distance away.

Because in futsal we quite often do not have enough time to perform a full dive, the splits tool is an extremely important skill to have. Personally, I feel as though this is why the younger the goalkeeper gets futsal specific training the better as this is when the body is much more flexible.

Once learning the skill, it is then a case of trying to use this in as many practices as you can, in different match-based contexts, and therefore this splits save will become more of an instinctive save rather than the goalkeeper having to think about doing it too much.

I only started learning to use the splits save at the age of 16 (but this is younger than most goalkeepers in this country) and so I then had to go through a stretching routine every morning for a good 3 months in order to feel comfortable doing the splits during games.

2) BRAVERY

You need an awful lot of bravery to be a goalkeeper in the first place, no matter what sport it is.

As everyone says, it can be the loneliest position on the pitch at times when things go wrong as it is such an individual object.

However, in futsal, I believe this is even more important but in slightly different ways. You must be prepared to use any part of the body possible to keep the ball out of the net.

In fact, coming to think of it, I can say the majority of my better saves in futsal have not come with my hands at all!

They mainly come from the body area or my feet due to the fast nature of the sport. The higher the level you are playing at, the braver and more inventive you must be.

It is almost a case of throwing out 90% of the conventional ways of saving and just purely thinking about keeping the ball out of the net because, at the end of the day, that's what goalkeeping is all about.

The number of times that a goalkeeper in futsal is put in a position where the odds are heavily weighed against them and they just throw themselves at the ball in a desperate attempt to help the team is fairly big.

Additionally, a futsal ball is heavier than a football and the technique most favourably used at the top level is the toe poke. When the ball is toe poked is provides major problems for a goalkeeper.

The ball tends to gather speed as it comes to you and there is no back lift from the attacker.

This is particularly difficult in Futsal as most of our trigger points are based on a player's back lift so, when there is none it is a matter of a guessing game and backing your instincts and body shape, with bravery becoming all the more important – of course – as there is no opportunity to shape or protect yourself when making the save.

3] CONFIDENCE

In futsal, clean sheets are like gold dust. Very rarely will you have the chance to keep a clean sheet and so it's a case of having the confidence of coming back from the opposition scoring a goal.

This was particularly hard for me at first, coming from a football background where you can pride yourself on keeping clean sheets on a regular basis.

In futsal, we're lucky (or good!) to keep two or three clean sheets in a season, so you can understand how the confidence element is vital.

4) DISTRIBUTION

This is massive in futsal due to the number of times you are in possession of the ball. Quite often, when you receive the ball, there is a set piece and this triggers what you do as a goalkeeper.

If your distribution is not good enough, then you not only harm your team's chances of attacking but - due to the small size of the pitch - it can also effect the team's chances of defending also and lead more readily to an opposition chance.

There are many types of different distribution in futsal as there are variants depending on the situation and the player you are passing to.

In terms of throwing, we have to judge whether the player will want the ball with pace or not, as well as what foot will the player want to receive the ball with and other factors like that...

People underestimate how much training and hard work goes into the distribution side of things; it is something that, as goalkeepers, we need to work on a huge amount regularly to maintain our form.

5) COMMUNICATION

Communication is extremely important and, yet, in some very different ways to the football goalkeeper.

In goalkeeping, there is always an emphasis on communication however in futsal it is seen in a different way. You must be loud and clear with your communication but you must not also give too much information when communicating.

The information must be clear, concise and straight to the point. The game is far too fast and will pass you by if you are too busy constantly talking and trying to make yourself known as I see some football goalkeepers like to do.

I've seen quite a few goalkeepers being caught out by talking whilst a shot has sneaked in!

Whilst communication at the right time is obviously crucial, it's all about being clever as a goalkeeper and knowing when – and how – to communicate most effectively.

GOALKEEPING IN BUSINESS

From gloves to rebound nets to goalkeeper coaching communities, the world of goalkeeping is rife with brands doing their best to help support the world of goalkeeping, innovate new products and generally develop your performance between the sticks. Often with very interesting stories that follow them, we've been lucky enough to catch up with the UK managers at brands such as Crazy Catch, Reusch and gloveglu.... Hear what they have to say in this section!

Represented in more than 20 countries from the UK and the US to Australia and Singapore, goalkeepers all around the world have embraced this unique, functional and affordable glove spray, bringing that extra bit of grip to the goalkeepers game. We caught up with their founder, Paul Sherratt, to find out a little more about the product, how it all began and how we, as goalkeepers, can use it to improve our game...

What was the idea behind GloveGlu? When did it all begin?

First, we asked ourselves a very fundamental question: why can't we produce a spray that can be applied to any level of goalkeeping gloves, from the professional-level right down to the bottom latex grades, to make them sticky?

After all, it's OK spending £100+ on gloves where the grip is great but the latex doesn't last very long at all. Conversely, if you spend £5 on a cheap pair, the gloves will last forever but the grip is non-existent. We stuck with the idea a little bit, and soon realised that this could prove to be a great opportunity.

So the journey began...

I contacted a friend of mine who has been working in the sports trade for nearly as long as I have (just short of 25 years!) and is also an expert in chemical applications on materials.

One of the key elements to creating the product was to ensure that the 'stickiness' was not too great that it meant that, every time you dived, the gloves picked up dirt and grass and not so subtle that it made no difference – an incredibly thin line!

We used our numerous contacts within the goalkeeping world (through both the professional and amateur ranks) to test the various strengths and, eventually, after 12 months of development and testing we cracked it, or so we thought...

Unfortunately there was one slight problem: The liquid was highly flammable! This, of course, had a number of implications, not least the fact that it would be very difficult to export the product and thus grow the business globally.

So, back to the drawing board and (finally) 6 months later gloveglu was launched in 2012 and has been going from strength to strength since then!

What is it about GloveGlu that makes it so attractive to goalkeepers around the world?

The most successful products are always the ones that are easy to understand.

Goalkeepers are always looking to ensure

FEATURED PRODUCT:

NAME:	gloveglu
TYPE:	GK GLOVE SPRAY
IDEAL FOR:	IMPROVING LATEX GRIP
LAUNCHED:	2012
SIZE:	N/A
PRICE:	£10.99

that their grip is good. This is why you see goalkeepers applying water to their gloves, spitting on them and coming up with their own concoctions.

GloveGlu really simplifies this process, making it easy to understand and without the 'risk factor' of using home remedies or something seen online... It's a specific product with specific advantages that goalkeepers at the highest level advocate too!

Another benefit is that it works with all types of latex on gloves, meaning there is no worry for goalkeepers as to whether the product might damage their gloves in the long-term or whether it just may not work at all; we were very clear about this when developing the spray...

How does the GloveGlu actually work – what's going on between the latex and the spray?

In simple terms, the gloveglu sits within the pores of the latex and acts as a 'reservoir' which feeds the latex with the gloveglu. Not only does this cause reinvigoration through additional moisture in the gloves (thus improving grip) but it also provides the latex with an adhesive element to further enhance that grip and support goalkeepers more.

Handily, this applies to both new and old gloves alike and – of course – whilst the

gloveglu spray will wear off over time, the beauty is that it can be easily reapplied with just another dose... Previously the only way to bring that grip back to life was to buy a whole new pair of gloves!!

You've obviously got your glove care range out at the minute too, but is there anything else on the way ?

For me, our product range has to solve problems or make the norm better: there's no point us doing it if not.

We have already identified a number of areas in goalkeeping and football where we believe we can create some better solutions, so you'll have to wait and see on that one...

It is this problem-solving element that drives the development and provides an additional level of enjoyment that we all thrive off and wish to take forward.

You can purchase your gloveglu spray today at www.gloveglu.com**!**

crazycatch®

It needs little more than to just utter the term 'Crazy Catch' at most junior cricket, football or goalkeeping training sessions for the children to jump up with excitement at the prospect of what's to follow... But it turns out there's a lot more to the innovative netting, designed by a sheep farmer, beyond the fact it comes readily assembled!

Tell us a little about how Crazy Catch was invented, who was at the heart of it all and how did it go from there?

Crazy Catch was invented in New Zealand by Andrew Sinclair. He was a sheep farmer and discovered that when you put two sheets of netting (sheep netting!) over each other, they created a fun and random rebound if you were to throw an object or ball against it.

This is the patented feature of the product and, whilst there are now other rebound nets sold around the world, none have the unique INSANE rebound produced by the two layers of netting overlapping.

Crazy Catch was born and originally was a cricketing product - you can find a good piece about the initial product making its TV debut on YouTube!

Fast forward to today and Crazy Catch is used by top athletes all around the world to improve their game. Most notably, the England Cricket, Hockey, Netball, Rugby and Football teams all use and advocate its athletic and skills-based development aid!

How have the rebound nets, as products, evolved since their launch?

The design has changed slightly over the years and the range has expanded quite considerably. The original Crazy Catch, as used by Brian Habana, was padded blue and with only a single side. Next came the black, two-sided designs, as well as a larger model called the 'Original' and then a smaller version, the 'Wildchild'.

In around 2008, the colours and range of the products were developed with the 'Professional', 'Wildchild' and 'Upstart' sizes added to the collection (at this time it was just a classic range so small netting on both sides - one single sheet of SANE netting, the other the patented INSANE double sheet).

The next innovation was a 'Double Trouble' range which came out in the UK in 2009. This range has the INSANE smaller netting plus a larger mesh which makes a football's reboundvery unpredictable. Now it's hugely popular in football with even Real Madrid using it regularly in their goalkeeper training.

In the future, we would like to make the nets more widely accepted as a training aid for outfield players, too, as there is definitely a great deal of touch/delivery work that can be done. This, of course, applies to goalkeepers

FEATURED PRODUCT:

NAME:	FREESTYLE
TPYE:	HAND-HELD REBOUND NET
IDEAL FOR:	CLOSE REFLEX SHOTS
LAUNCHED:	2012
SIZE:	0.5M X 0.5M
PRICE:	£50

too!

We also added the featured 'Freestyle' to our range in 2012, allowing a more direct approach to feeding/rebounds from coaches. Next up will probably be a glow in the dark Crazy Catch and possibly a much larger unit geared up for academies and clubs...

What skills can be trained with Crazy Catch and what do I need to get started?

Crazy Catch has a variety of benefits for goalkeepers: you can use it on your own to work on your skills or in larger club training sessions. It adds a new dimension and challenge to any drill, really, as the SANE side is great for repetition practices where you need a consistent feed. Practice claiming a high cross, handling skills, diving with a consistent feed all becomes possible and much easier, whilst the speed of the rebound can be increased by putting more pace on the feed.

The rebound speed does need to be experienced to be believed and this is one of the features that sets Crazy Catch apart as a leader and pioneering force in the industry. You can also develop your throwing and kicking accuracy, work on your control and improve first touch too...

Flip the product round onto the INSANE side and things get really interesting! The rebound is very unpredictable and

inconsistent. This tests your reactions and takes your game to the next level. Again this side of the net can be integrated into all kinds of training drills... limited only by your imagination!

Use a smaller ball, feed from different angles, change the angle of the Crazy Catch and instantly your training is different, more of a challenge and certainly more fun! Crazy Catch is a product loved by top-level international teams and clubs, such as Real Madrid and Leicester City, right down to very young athletes and goalkeepers, learning the movement of the ball and extra hand-eye coordination.

What is it about Crazy Catch that makes it so attractive to athletes across different sports and how can goalkeepers use it?

Even working with top international athletes, the thing that they always mention about training with Crazy Catch is how fun the product is to use! It really tests your reactions and skill level, adding an element of challenge and competition to any training session.

The speed of the rebound is always unexpectedly great the first time you throw a ball onto the net – it really pings back at you - and this is down to the quality of the design and manufacturing of the product.

The obvious benefit is skill development for ball sports... Being able to control, throw and catch accurately is a great way to improve your reactions, speed and agility, for example. However, there are also tonnes of hidden benefits, such as improving your vision, hand-eye coordination and decision making that can also be developed.

By training your eyes, your decision making as an athlete performing under pressure will improve and it's these little 1% details that the best athletes are constantly working on to ensure they are at their best. Within the world of goalkeeping, the uses and benefits are immeasurable which is why top, elite-level goalkeepers like Keylor Navas have used Crazy Catch to become one of the best in the world.

For coaches looking to add an element of fun and competition into their training sessions, this is certainly the way to go!

You offer a variety of different rebound nets... What's the difference from one to the next?

Crazy Catch is available in two distinct ranges. The 'Classic' range for small ball sports like cricket and hockey and the 'Double Trouble' range for big ball sports such as football. We have our handheld Freestyle product then 3 A-frame units: the Professional, the Wildchild and the Upstart

(available as either a classic version or double trouble version). The netting is the same on each model in terms of tension and size; it's just the frame size that varies.

How many different sports are there where Crazy Catch is used? What's the strangest?

Pretty much any ball sport can use Crazy Catch as a training aid, plus you have sports such as badminton and boxing where reactions and hand-eye coordination is key, so the product can be used to increase reactions and also visual performance and cognitive decision making.

Obviously the likes of cricket, football and hockey are the big ones, but the list is almost endless within the ball sport arena...

The strangest sport I have seen using Crazy Catch is something called VX International which, according to the BBC World Service, is "the best sport, you've never heard of"!!

You can visit www.crazycatch.com **to look through the ranges on offer as well as purchase your own rebound net for yourself, your club or your school!**

reusch®

The Reusch brand began nearly 80 years ago and yet is still standing as strong as ever today. We had a brief chat with UK manager Bob Filder and heard a little more about the history of Reusch as well as the various technologies employed within their gloves that may go unnoticed to you and me!

Reusch have been around for an incredibly long time: generations, in fact. Can you share with us the story of how it all started and reached where it is today?

In 1934, Karl Reusch manufactured his first pair of gloves in the attic of his home. With great passion, love for detail and the vision to create incomparable, innovative gloves of the highest possible quality, the first pairs of professional alpine ski gloves were sewn manually, by hand, and the Reusch brand, as we know it today, was born...

While developing and improving glove engineering for the alpine-skiing industry in 1972, Karl's son, Gebhard Reusch, joined forces with his father and Reusch entered the industry with a collection of specially designed winter gloves, expanding activities in their market.

Just one year later, in close co-operation with German goalkeeping legend Sepp Maier, Gebhard Reusch developed the first goalkeeper glove in history. A milestone for the world of soccer and Sepp Maier as well,

winning the World Cup just one year later.

Since 1974, more World Cups and European Championsips have been won by goalkeepers wearing Reusch gloves than any other glove brand. The plethora of awards won by Reusch gloves, whether on the ski track or the football field, simply cannot be understated. Now more than 80 years old, Reusch focuses purely on what it does best: producing top-quality football and ski gloves for amateurs and professionals.

Reusch is obviously a pretty big brand, but how big are we talking?

Reusch is a world market leader in the manufacturing of specialist goalkeeper and ski gloves with distributors in no less than 52 countries around the world.

Originating in Metzingen, Germany, and following a brief excursion to Valencia in Spain, Reusch International is now based within South Tyrol in Northern Italy in a town called Bolzano.

From there, the key elements of product design, brand marketing, athlete sponsorship and international logistics are controlled. Overall, the turnover in ski gloves is greater than in goalkeeper gloves but the HQ is very well-situated both at the bottom of the mountains and in Central Europe, making it easy to reach out to the abundant goalkeepers that Europe has to offer.

FEATURED GLOVES:

NAME:	RE:PULSE DELUXE G2
CUT:	DUAL ROLLED EXPANSE ESS
PALM:	G2 - ULTRASOFT
WRIST:	FULL STRAP W/ TEXTILE
SIZES:	7.5 - 11 (+12)
PRICE:	£50 - £95

What are the latest technologies employed within your gloves and how do they help to improve match performance?

Quite often, the technologies within our gloves are not obvious to the average goalkeeper but we constantly research and test new ideas with both professional and amateur goalkeepers to make even the most subtle and delicate of improvements or changes to improve the overall comfort and performance of each product.

Again, as a specialist brand, we offer different latexes to suit different playing surfaces and changeable weather conditions. We currently have 9 different latex palms available, to cover playing on different surfaces and weather conditions...

Moving on to the cuts, we offer all the different aspects available on the market as we try and produce products which suit all the different requirements based on personal choice, through playing surface and weather conditions.

Our list of in-glove technologies include:

- Ortho-Tec **(finger protection)**

- Pro Flex **(backhand flexibility)**

- Shockshield **(backhand/knuckle protection)**

- Expanded fingertips **(greater catching surface)**

- Airvent system **(improved breathability and ventilation)**

- Wrist Flex **(improve flexibility of wrist area)**

- Keep Control **(increase amount of latex on glove)**

- Catch Control **(silicone inserts on finger tips to increase grip)**

- 3D Thumb Crotch **(reduces tear chances in critca area)**

- Pull Loop **(making it easier to put on a second glove)**

These are just some of the key technologies which may not be immediately noticeable but help to give you that extra 1% when you need it most!

HO Soccer are renowned for bringing a new look and feel to goalkeeper gloves, worn by the likes of Burnley's Tom Heaton and West Ham's Adrián. They are famous for their elaborate style, which has catalysed the design of gloves throughout the goalkeeper world and given them an incredibly strong standing within the youth segment of the market...

How did HO Soccer emerge as a brand?

HO Soccer was formed in 2001 by two partners, Georges Martin and Jose Mendes, who established early on that there was a very poor selection of goalkeeping products at competitive prices in their respective countries of Portugal and Spain. Therefore, they set about creating the HO Soccer brand, which would produce and provide high-quality gloves but, most importantly, at affordable prices.

Has HO managed to expand outside of the continent much?

The size of the brand could be measured by its growth in the 15 years since it started... Gloves are now available in 35 countries across the world from Australia to Costa Rica and sponsors over 350 Professional goalkeepers worldwide, with new distributors in new markets joining every year. The gloves are made at our own factory and designs are generated at the Head Office in Spain before being shipped out to the eagerly awaiting young hands of the goalkeeping world!

Why are other firms not producing such colourful designs?

If you were to look at the major goalkeeping brands, you would see that they are all restricted by their corporate guidelines on design, which usually gives the brand a uniform strategy and image across their markets.

HO Soccer is unique in the sense that we can produce new, cutting-edge designs and colourways to keep up with the ever changing market more regularly.

Gloves like the Ghotta Gecko in Pink or Lime have been a huge success and the new Infinity collection of colours looks set to move on very promisingly.

What's the best way to get the most out of your gloves from a performance perspective?

With softer latex gloves you need to moisten the palm with water 30 minutes prior to the match and so "spit" only goes so far... Super soft latex can become slippery if over wet, so figure out the correct balance before the match so as to avoid wearing sponges when you need gripping power the most!

FEATURED GLOVES:

NAME:	LUNA GHOTTA INFINITY
CUT:	ROLL FINGER PALM
PALM:	AQUA CONTROL GRIP
WRIST:	ELASTIC WRIST WITH M.A.S
SIZES:	5 - 10.5
PRICE:	£64.99

To ensure your game gloves are in the best shape possible, don't practice with them. Buy an inexpensive training glove that can take the beating of training. Once your game gloves start to show signs of wear and tear, relegate them to the training pair and purchase a new pair for matches.

It's good practice to have at least one match pair and at least one training pair. Turf gloves are ideal for training in hard, dry conditions as they can take the rigorous pounding but will become slippery if the surface becomes wet.

Bulding on this, dirt and sweat break down the latex of the glove as dirt acts as sandpaper and dries the soft, tacky, porous latex into a hard crusty surface so rinsing the gloves after a game will help wash the spit, sweat and dirt away.

The gloves should be washed with lukewarm water and you should gently squeeze the excess water out.

What advice do you have to goalkeepers who are looking to become sponsored?

Many goalkeepers believe that they should or can be sponsored; this isn't the case. A brand will look at the request and will determine if this is a good business decision. The cost of sponsorship is expensive and so you need to see this from the brand's point of view as well:

How many more pairs of gloves will the brand sell by sponsoring you?

How much visibility will they get in the football world and does this outweigh the cost of free products?

You need to be honest in what you are looking for and honest in what you can do to help the brand... By saying that you are going to be the next England goalkeeper and they would be foolish not to support you isn't a great strategy!

WILLY CABALLERO

Willy is one of many goalkeepers through English football sponsored by HO Soccer. Currently plying his trade for Manchester City, Caballero was previously with Elche, Málaga and Boca Juniors. Famously, he saved 3 Liverpool penalties in the 2015 League Cup final to ensure victory for his team, despite previous criticisms.

Just4Keepers is an international goalkeeping school, spanning over 5 continents and with thousands of goalkeepers attending sessions on a weekly basis.

Spearheaded by ex-professional goalkeeper Ray Newland, the Just4Keepers story is certainly an interesting and inspiring one:

Your personal career was cut quite short by injury... Could you give us some insight, though, into what sort of level you were playing at before this?

I played most of my career in the second and third divisions of the Football League. Football life started briliantly for me when I was signed by ex-England goalkeeping legend Peter Shilton as he was player-manager at Plymouth Argyle...

I played for a few clubs and was in and out of the first team mainly because of injury (I never had one season where I missed less than 3 months through injury!).

There is only so long you can continue as a professional having recurring injuries each season and finally my luck ran out after 10 years, when a training ground injury whilst at Wigan finished my career.

In hindsight, I was lucky to have played for so long with my ongoing injuries and I

believe that - if I could have stayed injury free - I would have played consistently in the division two or three (modern-day Championship/League One).

When you founded J4K, what was the motivation: what were you trying to achieve?

In 1999, when I started J4K, the only place a young goalkeeper could go for specialised goalkeeper training was at a professional football club. As a professional goalkeeper I voluntarily coached at every club I played for except one and one thing I hated was that children were just treated like a number and it was just a conveyor belt because these clubs only wanted the best.

I was sick to death of seeing young goalkeepers getting thrown on the scrap heap by coaches with huge egos who did not care about the children who saw the coaches as absolute idols!

Not impressed by this, I wanted to provide an environment where young goalkeepers could attend a goalkeeper training session, no matter of what ability level, and develop whilst having fun but - more importantly - in an environment with no pressure on the children to perform. So this is why I started J4K.

Ray Newland
J4K Founder

What coaching qualifications do you have and how do you make sure you're always learning as a coach?

For the first 7 years of doing J4K, I did not have any coaching qualification because I believed what I had done in my career was more of an advantage to my students if I could pass on my experiences.

Also, over my 10 years as a goalkeeper, I was taught by 5 top ex-international goalkeepers and I wrote down every session I did with these legends and this is what I passed on to my students.

I now have my Level 3 Scottish Goalkeeper badge because I do think it is important to keep up with new techniques etc..

However, what I think is more important where we coach at J4K (the grassroots level) is helping our students develop their confidence and teach them with group training drills all whilst having fun.

Now, do not get me wrong: some of our sessions are intense and we do cater for all levels, but what we do at J4K is develop our goalkeepers so they are ready for academy football...

How we coach at J4K is more athlete-centred. If you take a look at the results we must be doing something right!

This is, of course, also down to the J4K coaches that put in such hard work to help their students, the parents for taking their students consistently – giving J4K time to develop them! - and also the goalkeepers for having the dedication to develop their goalkeeping.

What sort of sacrifices and risks have you experienced along the way and how do you feel about these looking back?

I have played in goal since I was 8 years old, so goalkeeping has been my life. I just want to give young goalkeepers the opportunity to achieve their dreams and give them the opportunities that I never had.

I have worked incredible hard to get J4K where it is, I have travelled quite a lot and probably my one regret is not spending more time off and going on holidays with my family.

From a risks perspective, I do not see what I have done with J4K as risky because I have such a passion for J4K and helping young goalkeepers that, if J4K stopped operating as coaching company, I would probably still do this for free anyway because goalkeeping is my passion, so I just do not see the risk in doing something you love.

ABOUT THE AUTHOR...

Adam is a 16-year-old author, goalkeeper and entrepreneur from Aylesbury, Buckinghamshire. Having been frustrated by the quality of coaching, debate and similar information on goalkeeping, he decided to write this (his third book) around 6 months ago.

He attends Aylesbury Grammar School and is an avid Oxford United fan, whislt also playing handball to a representative standard with East England.

With a passion for all things development, learning and goalkeeping, the book was the perfect opportunity for Adam to research deeper into the world of goalkeeping and pick up invaluable life skills, contacts and experiences along the way.

Previous titles include 'FIFA 15: A Game Without Limits' and '135 Things to Write Lists About', although his latest project commands a much higher calibre than the previous two, not just because he has had the opportunity to work on the project full-time for the last couple of months after the GCSE period.

Interested in a career enveloping aspects of coaching, business and journalism, Adam is always open to further opportunities, whether on the coaching field, in the studio or over the internet, to gain experience and knowledge; any thoughts can be emailed over to the contact details aforementioned and we'll see if there is something that we can work.